Living in the Highlands

Saw this and
thought of you – what
a lonely time we shared in
Westn Ross last year –
Love to you both –
Susan July. 2001

LESLEY ASTAIRE · RODDY MARTINE

Living in the Highlands

Photographs by ERIC ELLINGTON

With 204 color illustrations

Thames & Hudson

For Rocky and Patty

Half title. *A young piper at the Portree Highland Games on Skye.*
Title Page: *Plaid throws from Anta at Ballone Castle, Portmahomack,*
Easter Ross.

Right: *A clear day on Loch na Dal on the island of Skye where the sea*
sweeps in from the Sound of Sleat.

On the contents pages. Left: *Family crest of the Macpherson-Grant*
family of Ballindalloch. Right: *The Armoury at Inveraray Castle, Loch*
Fyne; Ploughman's Hall, Old Rayne; Anta Ceramics in Easter Ross;
Ballindalloch Castle, Spey Valley

Texts © 2000 Thames & Hudson Ltd, London
Photographs © 2000 Eric Ellington

First published in hardcover in the United States of America
in 2000 by Thames & Hudson Inc, 500 Fifth Avenue,
New York, New York 10110

ISBN 0-500-01986-X
Library of Congress Catalog Card Number 99-69291

Printed and bound in China by Everbest Printing Co., Ltd.

Contents

Foreword By His Grace the Duke of Argyll

Inveraray Castle,
Argyll

As the title suggests, living in the Highlands of Scotland can give the impression to those who do not that we must exist in a veritable earthly Paradise, surrounded by the most magnificent scenery, a miraculous juxtaposition of lochs, rivers and hills all bedecked with truly God-given flaura and fauna in profusion, with a climate to match these idyllic conditions.

I can assure the reader that much of the above is true, as is revealed in this superb book so perceptively written by the author and gloriously illustrated by Eric Ellington.

Whilst you will delight in the various chapters of some of our lives, objectives, indeed ambitions, do keep in mind at all times that what is presented to you has not come at all easily. Our forebears and to some extent ourselves have had to climb some pretty steep hills to be here at all today.

Our much-loved land has never been rich in material resources; agriculture and fishing, which would seem such natural pursuits for this type of terrain and climate, have had to be fought for every inch of the way -- which is possibly why the Scot has evolved into the rather special person that is the species today.

We have to be innovative in every endeavour we pursue. To that end we recognize and reward talent, which is often the envy of the world, be it in engineering, medicine, banking, architecture. This most probably stems from the emphasis we have always instilled into the next generation ... being a sound and all-embracing education.

Despite the underlying Calvinist ethos, we very much enjoy life; and the remarkably beautiful trappings that can be found the length and breadth of this small part of the Kingdom, as has been so well shown in this book, reflect the vast palette of what we have and our desire to share it with others.

Introduction

The northernmost mainland area of Scotland is a region of high mountains, deep lochs and dark moorland, a breakaway, dessicated plateau of ancient rocks forming glens and lochs carved by long ago ice floes. The consequent mountain ranges, Monadhliath, Grampian and Cairngorm, all rise to approximately the same height above sea level, with deep water canyons and heather-clad open spaces in between.

Traditionally, the Highlands of Scotland begin above a range of hills, the Campsie Fells and the Ochils, which stretch from north of Glasgow on Scotland's west coast to the cut of the Firth of Tay and Strathmore on the east. Until the 18th century there were no roads here, the great herds of small black cattle from the far north and islands of the west being brought across mountain tracks, which became known as Drove Roads, to the markets of Perth, Comrie, Crieff, Stirling and Dumbarton, and later Edinburgh and Glasgow.

It was an inhospitable landscape which even the Roman legions of the early part of the millennium backed away from, and by the 14th century the Highlands had become largely divided up into clan territories with land-holdings of tribes or families who gave their allegiance to a Scottish king, or Ard Righ, and a south of Scotland-based seat of government first at Stirling and Dunfermline, then Edinburgh.

In many ways this suited Highlanders and Lowlanders alike, the latter coming to regard the former as wild men and savages. Such was the difficulty of communication and travel in this largely hostile territory that Highland chiefs could rule with virtual autonomy, and much of their time was taken up with survival. As a consequence, inter-clan feuds were commonplace and clan castles were always designed with defence purposes in mind.

Although Scottish kings regularly took steps to curtail the excesses of the Highland chiefs, by the early 18th century they had reached their zenith. Following two Jacobite risings, when large numbers of clansmen

rose up to support the *de jure* Stuart claimants to the British throne, exiled for their Catholic faith, a London-based government at long last came to the conclusion that they would have to take steps to curtail the power of the chiefs who by this stage in their history were able to field their own army, should they choose to.

Following the Battle of Culloden Moor in 1745, when those who had risen up in support of Prince Charles Edward Stuart were finally decimated by the British Army, which included both Highland and Lowland Scots who did not share the Jacobite persuasion, Highland life was to radically change. The patronage of the chiefs was broken, many sent into exile, and Field Marshal George Wade was despatched north from England to build roads and to open up the remoteness of the glens and mountain passes.

Opposite: *The flat lands of the Isle of Skye with the Cuillins towering beyond.*

Above left: *Water tumbles through the forest of Glen Tanar in Aberdeenshire.*

Above right: *The River Isla at Keith in winter spate.*

Above: *A seascape in Wester Ross where the salt water cuts inland to create a landscape of unsurpassed beauty.* Below: *A tractor stands by on crofting land.* Right: *A churchyard lies abandoned and lonely beside Loch Duich, which stretches from the head of Loch Alsh in Wester Ross.*

Sheep graze on a headland on the Isle of Skye. In the far distance can be seen the Scottish mainland.

Opposite: *Steps lead into the courtyard of Duart Castle on the Isle of Mull, where a Rowan tree wards off evil spirits.*

The uprising, it should be appreciated, had greatly shocked the British Government of the day, not least because at one stage it had appeared unstoppable. The question therefore was how to make sure that a rebellion of this kind in the far north of Britain could never occur again?

The answer was to irreparably reform the old ways of Highland life, particularly to challenge the outmoded allegiances owed by the tenantry to their clan chiefs. It was a devious and cleverly commercial initiative. Landowners, often newcomers who had moved in to purchase land as the Jacobites fled into exile, were soon persuaded that the only viable future for land ownership in the Highlands lay in sheep farming.

But to be fair, there was another aspect to such thinking which was powerfully influenced by the politicially well-intentioned 'agrarian improvers' of the 18th and 19th centuries. Contrary to the romanticized image it has acquired in more recent times, crofting was a poor and often

A portrait of Lord Maclean, 27th Chief of Clan Maclean, who seems to gaze through a window in the Banqueting Hall of Duart Castle.

Opposite: *A classic Highland estate nestles in the wooded landscape of Donside in Aberdeenshire.*

wretched way of life. You only have to read the accounts given by Martin Martin in his *Description of Western Isles*, written in 1703, or the accounts given by Dr Samuel Johnson and James Boswell of their tour of Scotland and the Hebrides in 1773, to formulate a picture of what conditions were like.

The land, largely peat bog, mountain and moor, offered a meagre existence against a wildly variable climate. When Dr Johnson made his celebrated sojourn, he visited the ancestors of three of the families who appear in this book, among them Sir Allan Maclean of Duart. To Sir Allan he made the following harsh observation: 'Your country consists of two things: stone and water. There is indeed a little earth above the stone in some places, but very little, and the stone is always appearing. It is like a man in rags, the naked skin is always peeping through.'

Although Dr Johnson was later to describe his foray into the Highlands as the pleasantest part of his life, what he saw, with the notable exception of Inveraray, lacked the sophistication he so very much cherished. And for a century thereafter, as British eyes looked across the Atlantic Ocean and beyond, acquisitive for New World territory in the build-up of Empire, men, women and children from the Highland crofting communities filtered into a steady flow of emigration, while the land they left behind was rapidly colonized by a hardy breed of sheep imported from the Cheviot Hills in the Scottish Borderland.

As a result of the enforced and voluntary exodus which then took place, the already comparatively small populations of Perthshire, Argyll, Inverness, Ross and Cromarty, Caithness and Sutherland, instead of growing with the rest of Scotland, dropped by over 60,000 in the space of eighty years.

The depopulation of Strathglass, for example, gives a picture of what took place across the region. In 1801, no less than 799 Clan Chisholm tenants were forced to sail from Fort William for Pictou in Nova Scotia. The following year, a further 473 departed for Upper Canada and 128 for Pictou. At Knoydart, 55 departed upon another ship, and in 1803, four ships carrying 480 also left for Pictou. In the space of three years, therefore, 5,390 people were obliged to vacate Strathglass and Glen Urquhart.

The countless piles of rubble scattered throughout the northern glens where the crofts and shielings once stood bear testimony to this. But the

particular irony is that while the true Highlanders were being driven from their homes, or leaving of their own accord for the prospect of a better life, the rest of Scotland was becoming increasingly fascinated by their romantic history in a desperate desire to create a national identity.

When launched by their author James Macpherson in the 1760s, the nowadays discredited poems of Ossian, which revelled in Celtic antiquity, captivated the public imagination, both in Britain and across Europe. The poetry of Robert Burns and the period novels of Sir Walter Scott inspired not only their own generations, but those that followed. And it only needed Queen Victoria and her husband, the Prince Consort, to establish a foothold in Aberdeenshire in the mid-19th century for a resurgence of fashionable interest to take place. From the moment Prince Albert signed the lease of the Deeside castle of Balmoral, which he subsequently purchased and rebuilt, the Highlands of Scotland were reinvented as a sporting playground for the well-to-do. Not necessarily welcomed by

The town of Oban crowned by McCaig's Folly (a 19th-century replica of the Colosseum in Rome), which was funded by a local businessman to provide local employment, but never completed. Below it sits the town's distillery which produces a splendid single malt whisky.

Opposite: *Performers and spectators at the Portree Highland Games on Skye.*

everybody, it brought with it an influx of wealth and patronage which, had it not taken place, might have left unstemmed the departure of young blood in search of something better.

Instead of fortified castles and keeps, wealthy Victorians acquired land to build mansions and shooting lodges to indulge themselves, and their friends, with the abundant availability of sport, stalking and fishing. Within a decade or so, an annual autumn sojourn into the Highlands became *de rigueur* for the socially aspirant following the lead set by the British Royal Family.

To entertain their houseparties, a series of traditional Scottish games came into being, followed by Highland balls with Scottish country dancing. To a degree, although everybody recognized that it could never aspire to being the same, the trappings of clanship, glossily exaggerated, enjoyed a revival.

The incoming families, many of whom were unable to boast any great Highland antiquity, but who had ridden on the crest of the great industrial revolution of the 19th and early 20th centuries, immediately set about acquiring their own tartans to enact the imagery of the Highland laird. With the wealth they had accumulated from trade in the Far East, shipping on the Clyde, tea investment in India and railways across America, they built mock Gothic mansions in Highland beauty spots to emphasize their self-importance. The practice continues to this day, albeit on a smaller scale.

Alongside this, however, the towns and villages prospered, not only on the mainland, but on the chain of western islands today linked by regular ferry crossings. In these Inner and Outer Hebrides, the native language of Gaelic has prevailed, and despite recent economic setbacks, the population continues to thrive, but the future inevitably lies in individual enterprise to prevent the young from moving away. The advent of an outpost department of the University of the Highlands, based at Stornoway on the island of Lewis, could prove just the catalyst that is required to reverse the trend.

Tremendous changes were to take place in the Highands during the course of the 20th century. There are still vast areas of land devoted to sheep farming, and large sporting estates continue to survive by leasing out their stalking and fishing, but it is the quality of life to some extent created by the spin-off from such activities that has become the main attraction.

Crofting, for example, has also been making something of a comeback, though most crofters nowadays hold down other jobs to make it pay. Even the more radical politicians have been forced to admit that the romance surrounding the 'but and ben' existence, so predominent in Highland folklore, requires large sums of public subsidy to sustain it. Introduced in the 1960s, the Highlands & Islands Development Board, superseded by Highlands & Islands Enterprise, has made significant progress in encouraging new business projects, simultaneously supporting existing employers.

Developments in communications technology have helped a number of small businesses to set up in some unlikely locations, but it is in the two largest Highland conurbations that the new-found prosperity is most evident. Inverness, through its strategic location, is the undisputed

Highland capital. Situated as the River Ness flows from Loch Ness into the Moray Firth, it marks the eastern approach to the remarkable Caledonian Canal which follows the natural fault line through Loch Oich and Loch Lochy to Fort William on the west coast.

There has been a town here for approaching 900 years, although few original buildings have survived, the majority having been constructed of wood. Inverness Castle itself dates from 1836 but occupies the site of much older fortifications. A startling contrast in architectural style is evident with the glass-fronted Eden Court Theatre, completed in 1976, which houses the arts centre for the region, staging concerts, exhibitions and theatre.

Not the most attractive of towns, being too much of a mix of the traditional and modern, Inverness is nevertheless the shopping centre for the region, growing steadily with small industrial estates fringing the out-skirts. Aberdeen, however, situated on the east coast, is a visual delight.

A lace maker at work in Pitsligo village on the east coast.

Right: *Fishing creels in a coastal village emphasize the strong economic importance of the sea in Highland life.*

Opposite: *The bustling harbour of Aberdeen, Oil Capital of the North.*

A seat of learning since the 15th century, King's College was founded by Bishop Elphinstone in 1494; and from the mid-18th century onwards, it was the quarrying of granite which put the city on the map. Both London Bridge and Waterloo Bridge in London were fabricated from Aberdeen stone and are enduring memorials to its quality.

As the British Empire expanded, shipbuilding developed, with Aberdeen becoming famous for fabricating the sharp-bowed 'clippers' specifically designed for the China Seas and for the transportation of emigrants to Australia. Since the 1970s, the city has prospered extensively from the spin-off from the discovery of oil and gas in the cold, deep waters of the North Sea.

The undeniable fact, however, is that the greater proportion of the Highland region consists of mountain, moor and peat bog which offer little commercial potential other than as a habitat for deer, although

commercial forestry has been widely introduced, not always to the benefit of the landscape or incumbent wildlife.

Agriculture, though suffering seriously in the aftermath of the beef crisis of the 1990s, continues to be a critical influence on the Highland economy, as does Scotch whisky distillation, particularly on Speyside. However, tourism is undoubtedly the greatest money-spinner, and by combining a sense of the past, old castles, clans and tartans, with sporting activities such as hill-walking, golf, sailing, pony-trekking and mountaineering during the summer, skiing and curling over the winter, there is plenty on offer.

Happily, standards of hospitality have risen perceptibly to meet the demand, with certain Highland hotels ranking among the best in the world. Then there is Scotland's natural larder to enjoy: Aberdeen Angus beef, venison from the hills, salmon and trout from the rivers, fresh lobster and prawns from the sea. Today Scottish fish farms and the attendant smokeries export throughout the world.

Encouraged by the growing visitor statistics, craft industries encompassing everything from textiles, weaving and leatherwork to pottery, wine-making and perfumery products have sprung up. If you add to this the spectacular nature and diversity of the landscape, the Highland region emerges as an incomparable destination – regardless of the weather.

For this book there has been an embarrassment of choice, this being such a vast region with so much going on in the most unlikely places. From the start, however, it was decided that it was important not to bring together simply another selection of elaborate, eclectic interiors, but to create a sense of lifestyle.

Therefore, all the people who feature in the following pages have a purpose to their existence, whether it is opening an ancestral home to the public to secure its future, creating a beautiful garden, contributing towards the well-being of a local community, or earning a living by manufacturing something either traditional or new.

All have chosen to live in the Highlands of Scotland for similar reasons, but most notably because it offers them that sense of freedom and tranquillity which no longer exists in the heavily populated urban centres of the south.

The Duke and Duchess of Argyll
at Inveraray Castle

1 *The Keeper of the Quaich*

The Duke and Duchess of Argyll. Behind them can be seen a portrait of the Duchess by John Merton.

Opposite: *Inveraray Castle from the south-west.*

It was while on duty with his regiment, the Argyll & Sutherland Highlanders, on the East/West German frontier in 1960 that the 12th Duke of Argyll, then Marquess of Lorne, began to wonder what he would do when he left the army. Concluding that most red-blooded Scots either build a golf course or sell Scotch whisky, he chose the latter project.

In 1969, therefore, when he returned to Inveraray Castle, his family's ancestral home on Loch Fyne in Argyll, he launched Argyll Whisky, his own brand, and a few years later was invited by Pernod Ricard, continental Europe's largest wines and spirits company, to join the board of its subsidiary company, Campbell Distillers Ltd.

In those days, most people tended to equate Scotch with blended whisky, because there were relatively few single malts available to the general public. It slowly became apparent, however, that consumers wanted something more, and the industry became convinced that one way of promoting its whiskies was to emphasize the flavours, surroundings and mysteries of the Highlands where it originated.

This initiative was then taken up by The Keepers of the Quaich, an exclusive organization created within the Scotch whisky industry to promote the interests and enjoyment of its products. The quaich is the ancient traditional drinking vessel of the Scottish people, a two-handled cup, usually made of wood, bone or silver; and today it provides a symbol for a world-wide fraternity of Scotch whisky drinkers.

As he had been a founder patron of The Keepers of the Quaich, it was entirely appropriate that in 1997 the Duke should serve for a year as the 9th Grand Master, a role which he greatly cherished, having helped the society grow in size and influence since its inception.

The Campbells of Argyll first came to prominence in the 13th century, their name derived from the Gaelic *cam-beul* meaning 'crooked mouth'. From their support of Robert the Bruce during the struggle for independence against the English, and subsequent strategic marriages,

Hand-painted garlands of flowers by Girard decorate the window shutters in the State Dining Room.

they gained extensive lands on the west coast as the influence of the Macdonald Lords of the Isles declined. Titles in the grant of 1701, in which the 10th Earl of Argyll was created Duke, reflect the clan territories - Duke of Argyll, Marquess of Kintyre and Lorne, Earl Campbell and Cowal, Viscount Lochow and Glenlya, Lord Inveraray, Mull, Morvern and Tiree.

Dukes of Argyll were also appointed Heritable Sheriffs of Argyll and Masters of the Royal Household in Scotland in 1464, Admirals of the Western Coasts and Isles of Scotland, and Keepers of the Castles of Dunstaffnage, Tarbert, Carrick and Dunoon. In 1996, Sir Ian Campbell, 12th Duke of Argyll, was appointed Lord Lieutenant of Argyll.

In the Highlands of Scotland, however, the Duke insists that his most widely honoured title is that of Mac Cailein Mor, which translates from the Gaelic as 'Son of Colin the Great', a tribute to his ancestor of 800 years ago. He and his Duchess, the former Iona Colquhoun of Luss, were married in 1964, and have a son, the Marquess of Lorne, and a daughter, Lady Louise Burrell.

From early April until the end of October each year, Inveraray Castle is open to the public. Like all great Scottish mansions, it reflects a variety of styles introduced by succeeding generations. Most of the present-day building was completed for the 5th Duke in 1773, when the entire old town of Inveraray was replaced by a model new town on the loch foreshore. To achieve this, the original plans for the castle and town, which had been drawn up earlier by the English architect Sir John Vanbrugh, were adapted by the Palladian exponent Peter Morris and overseen by William Adam, himself father of Scotland's most remarkable family of innovative architects. Robert Mylne, the master mason responsible for many of Scotland's great houses, was later brought in to recast the castle interiors during the 1780s.

Then a century later, the upper floors of the castle were gutted by fire, and Anthony Salvin, the Victorian castle expert, was consulted. It was he who suggested the conical roofs on the exterior corner towers, and who also redesigned the central tower as the Armoury Hall that can be seen today.

Earlier, in 1871, the 8th Duke of Argyll's heir, the Marquess of Lorne, had married Princess Louise, Queen Victoria's fourth daughter, and to

Opposite: *the Armoury Hall, in which a variety of historical Highland weapons are exhibited.*

Above left: *A display of 16th- and 17th-century pole arms.*

Above right: *Painted wall panel in the State Dining Room.*

mark the occasion, Matthew Digby Wyatt had been invited to design an elaborate glass and iron entrance bridge.

Ravaged once more by fire in 1975, the Castle was again extensively renovated. Twenty tons of scaffolding were employed in the restoration of the central towers, and the entire house has been re-lined, re-pointed, plastered and painted in the authentic 18th-century manner.

The result is a magnificent showpiece that not only reflects the status of one of Scotland's most important dynasties, but also encapsulates the style and triumphalism of Scotland following the 1707 Act of Union with England.

The State Dining Room with German silver-gilt sailing ships or 'nefs' as table decorations. Opposite: *The magnificent Tapestry Drawing Room with its original set of Beauvais tapestries.*

The Duke of Argyll is a founder patron of The Keepers of the Quaich, and is a former Grand Master of the Society.

Right: *An overview of Inveraray Castle and town looking south across Loch Fyne.*

2 *March of the Highland Men*

Highland games might be compared with English village fetes. They are essentially social and community-led, and often indulge ancient traditions. But there the similarity ends. These games and gatherings have their origins in the violent and bloody clan and political conflicts of Scotland's turbulent history. At their most simplistic, they are trials of strength dating back to the 11th century when King Malcolm Canmore (he who in Shakespeare's Scottish play terminated and supplanted King Macbeth) summoned his 'hardiest soldiers' and 'fleetest messengers' to the Braes of Mar. These men, tough by any standards, were invited to compete against each other to test their potential in battle.

With the advent of the clan system, which largely took place from the 13th century onwards, local contests modelled on those featured in the Braes of Mar experiment were given a new significance, and have taken place in and around the mainland and island towns and villages ever since. With the exodus of Highlanders into the lowlands of Scotland and beyond, there are nowadays approximately 100 such organized events taking place in Scotland every year, and countless others throughout the world.

Gatherings vary in size, with local folk mingling freely with tourists. The traditional sports – tossing the caber, putting the shot or stone, hill-running, throwing the hammer and Highland dancing and piping competitions – now rank alongside cycle racing, sheep-dog trials and the recently introduced haggis hurling.

Best known of the traditional sports, of course, is probably caber tossing, once known as 'ye casting of ye bar'. It is said to derive from the time foresters cast their logs into the deepest part of a river so that the current would carry them swiftly downstream. Whatever the true origin,

The Lonach Highlanders march proudly onto the games field for the annual Lonach Gathering.

Competitors in the Highland dancing.

Opposite clockwise: *Putting the Shot, Tossing the Caber, and sharing a dram of Scotch whisky with friends.*

caber tossing is recorded as far back as the 16th century, not only in Scotland but in Germany, Sweden, France and Italy. Even the much-married Henry VIII of England, in his youth considered the finest athlete in his realm, had a go at it.

Another of the most popular sports is the tug-o'-war. Local teams, often with as many competitors as 100 on each side, try to topple their opponents by pulling on a great rope. Although largely amateur in nature, some competitors have acquired professional status and today travel the world as champions of their specific sport.

The Lonach Gathering at Bellabeg in Strathdon, which dates from 1835, is not the oldest of Highland Games, but it is certainly one of the more colourful. In fact, the Lonach Gathering Society, which continues to run the event, was formed twelve years earlier in 1823, and since then has proved a remarkable catalyst for the local community. Originally comprising those who gave allegiance to the local hierarchy, notably Clan Forbes, but also the Wallaces and the Gordons, now one has to have lived in the area and be between 18 and 30 years old to qualify for membership, or be the son of a member (in which case 16 is the lowest qualifying age). The Lonach Gathering Society, although its purpose is to organize the Games,

Above and Opposite: *The skirl of the pipes. Pipe bands annually travel from all over the world to put in an appearance on the Scottish Highland Games circuit.*

is essentially a charitable foundation, using its funds to provide pensions and assistance for members over 70, widows and disabled members.

And what makes the Lonach Gathering even more special is that it is the last such event in the Highlands after the Royal Braemar Gathering to maintain the March of the Highland Men, very much a feature of such occasions in the past. Around 110 of a membership of approximately 180 take part, setting off to call on the big houses of the district in turn, where the age-old tradition is that the lairds welcome them with a dram.

Dressed in distinctive green jackets and bonnets, and the Forbes and Wallace tartans, accompanied by the Gordon sett of the Lonach Pipe Band, the uniforms are offset by the tartans of the invited guest pipe bands such as Towie, Ballater & District, or Buchan & District. The March of the Highland Men is always a splendid sight to behold.

Oliver and Clare Russell
at Ballindalloch Castle

3 *An Aberdeen Angus tradition*

*Clare and Oliver Russell in their
private sitting room.*

Opposite: *Above a window under the
roof is a carving of the cat symbol of
Clan Macpherson on top of the initials
of Sir George Macpherson-Grant,
placed there by his son in 1850.*

Aberdeen Angus, Scotland's most renowned breed of cattle, is
famous throughout the world, and the oldest herd in continuous
existence is to be found at Ballindalloch Castle, in the fertile surroundings
of the Spey Valley. Clare Russell, who inherited the estate from her father,
Sir Ewan Macpherson-Grant in 1979, maintains the herd which was first
created by her great-grandfather in 1860. This beautiful race of cattle is
directly descended from the native cattle found in the north-east of
Scotland and derives its origins from the old 'Doddies' of Angus and the
'Hummlies' from Buchan. They were all hardy black hornless cattle who
thrived well on grass and produced the best quality meat. The magnificent
stock bull is shared with the Queen Mother's herd at the Castle of Mey
in Caithness.

Over the centuries, Ballindalloch Castle has earned itself the title of
the 'Pearl of the North'. But it was not always so. Like many another great
Highland mansion, it was originally built in the 16th century for defence.
The exact date when the original tower house was erected is not known,
but the date 1546 is carved on a stone lintel in one of the bedrooms.
Constructed on the traditional Z-plan design, the building seen today has
been much altered and enlarged.

A legend exists that it was to have been built on the hill above its
present location. Certainly the foundations of such a building can be seen
to this day. But the story goes that the Laird built the Castle three times
on this site and three times it was blown mysteriously to the ground. The
third time, during a mighty gale, a ghostly voice was heard to repeat:
'Build it in the coo-haugh', and that is where it stands today.

The branch of the Grant family who settled at Ballindalloch were to
prosper until the early 18th century when financial problems compelled
them to sell the estate to their cousin Colonel William Grant, commander
of one of the independent Highland regiments from which the Black
Watch was formed. His cousin was the distinguished soldier, General

A detail of the plasterwork in the fan-vaulted hall, designed by Thomas Mackenzie as part of the 1850s renovation.

Right: *The library, which contains 2,500 volumes, providing a three-dimensional history of the cultural, literary and artistic development of the family. The 19th-century Drum Table is unusually tall, but in proportion to the high ceilings.*

James Grant, who fought in the American War of Independence and became Governor of Florida in 1763. Inheriting Ballindalloch in 1770, he built the north wing especially to house his favourite French chef. On his death, the estate was inherited by George Macpherson of Invereshie, his nephew, who in 1838 was created a baronet, with the title Sir George Macpherson-Grant of Ballindalloch.

When Clare's parents, Sir Ewan and Lady Macpherson-Grant, inherited the castle they made several modernizations, such as placing a new kitchen next to the dining room, installing eight bathrooms and re-wiring and re-roofing the entire building. This work was completed in 1967, the year in which Clare and Oliver were married.

Today Ballindalloch Castle is open to visitors, and Clare herself has created several unique features, such as a family nursery room full of toys belonging to her ancestors, which she came across stored in an attic. She has created a romantic rose garden within the old walled garden to celebrate the Castle's 450th anniversary.

In the grounds a gentle waterfall runs through the rock garden, at the foot of which is a rock pool, into which coins are thrown by visitors and passed on to the Children's Hospice Association (Scotland).

The sense of continuity and being a family home is apparent from the moment you arrive at Ballindalloch Castle, and Oliver and Clare's children, sons Guy and Edward and daughter Lucy, now grown up, return regularly. Guy, the eldest, has changed his name to Macpherson-Grant to ensure that the family tradition continues.

Left: *The dining room is the largest room in the castle. It was redesigned and panelled in American pine, and the design of the ceiling was fashionably copied from casts taken from Craigievar Castle in Aberdeenshire. Above the fireplace is the coat of arms of the Macphersons and the Grants, displaying the two clan mottos: 'Ense et Animo' for the Grants, and 'Touch not the Cat Bot a Glove' for the Macphersons. The carpet is Persian, and the large painting on the right is of Queen Charlotte by Allan Ramsay. The silver cups were won by Sir George Macpherson-Grant, 3rd Baronet, for his world-famous herd of Aberdeen Angus cattle.*

Above: *A writing desk sits by a window in the fan-vaulted hall.*

Family portraits and photographs.

Right: *The nursery represents a history of 'young lairds and lassies' from the late 18th century to modern times. There is a collection of much-loved 19th- and 20th-century dolls, and the modern doll's house was made by Oliver Russell for his daughter Lucy in 1975.*

The magnificent stone doorway was carved in 1850 and above it can be seen
the Macpherson and Grant coat of arms and the inscription, 'The Lord shall
preserve thy going out and coming in' (taken from the 121st Psalm).
Left: Ballindalloch boasts one of Scotland's finest herds of Aberdeen Angus cattle,
which during the summer months graze close to the castle. The herd was started
by Clare Russell's great-grandfather, Sir George Macpherson-Grant, and
flourishes today under farm manager Robert Shiach, M.B.E.

An Aberdeen Angus tradition 51

Lachlan and Annie Stewart
at Ballone Castle

4 *A childhood dream*

The Stewart family gather at Ballone Castle for Annie's birthday party.

Opposite: *Under extensive repair, the Castle stands on a headland of Tarbet Ness, south of Portmahomack between the Dornoch Firth and the Moray Firth.*

It started when Lachlan Stewart was a schoolboy and first set eyes upon the ruins of Ballone Castle, a 16th-century fortified tower on the shoreline of Easter Ross. He was staying with a schoolfriend who lived nearby, and would often go to look at the old ruin. He knew even then that one day he would own it and make it his home.

But that was over thirty years ago

Lachlan and Annie met at Edinburgh College of Art during the 1970s. When they graduated, they married and moved to London where they launched Anta, taking the name from a Greek word meaning Column. 'There was no special sigificance,' says Lachlan. 'We just liked the sound of it.' Within months Anta's tartan tableware was attracting large orders from New York, and as their business expanded, the Stewarts decided to return to Scotland and set up a factory.

Lachlan had always harboured an affection for the north-east coast, and taking Annie on a walk to Tarbet Ness one day, discovered that Ballone Castle was still in ruins.

'I had heard it was to be restored,' he says. 'I couldn't believe it was still as I remembered it.'

After a visit to the farmer who owned the land upon which the Castle stood, and various negotiations thereafter, Lachlan and Annie found themselves the owners of a derelict castle. Slowly, but surely, they have been putting it to rights, but at the same time the demand for Anta's products, plates, mugs, saucers and tartan throws, has been increasing, with regular outlets in Japan and America, as well as a growing home market.

Since moving and establishing their workshop and a shop at Fearn, a short distance away from Ballone, Lachlan and Annie and their three children, Lachlan junior, Archie and Stella, have been living in a purpose-built shed. Following the opening of an Edinburgh shop in the summer of 1997, Lachlan and Annie decided to throw a celebration. And what better place to hold it in than Ballone Castle?

There was only one problem. Although a tremendous amount of work has already been done at Ballone, it did not at that point have a roof. The Stewarts decided to go ahead anyway, and since the repairs were not yet completed they let it be known that the party was to celebrate Annie's fortieth birthday.

Since Portmahomack is at the heart of Clan Gordon farming country, virtually everybody invited had the surname of Gordon, and everybody

Trestle tables with linen cloths were laid out for the birthday party in the Castle's banqueting hall. Guests joined in the spirit of the occasion, serving themselves with Anta plates and beakers.

brought something with them to contribute to the feast. So as not to be outdone, one neighbour called Chris Swift even brought a whole stag.

The Stewarts gave each guest an Anta plate and an Anta beaker, and then left them to fend for themselvs. After dinner there was traditional Scottish country dancing to an accordion band.

Tartan rugs and throws, and plaid carpet and bedspread, add colour and warmth to the principal bedroom. An Orkney chair stands in a corner.

A childhood dream 55

Left: *Anta cups and bowls on display in the Anta shop beside a curtain of plaid throws.*

Above: *Ceramics are decorated by hand in the workshop.*

Lynda Usher
at Glen Urquhart

5 *More of a gallery than a shop*

Ten miles west of Inverness is Beauly, a planned village laid out in the 1840s by the 12th Lord Lovat, whose castle stands nearby. Valliscaulian monks built a priory here in 1230 and, being French-speaking, called it 'Beau lieu' meaning 'beautiful place'. The ruins of their priory can still be seen, and Beauly, having moved on from being a community dependent upon the patronage of 'church and laird', still remains a beautiful place.

Lynda Usher began her career as a knitwear designer, having trained at the Royal College of Art in London. Setting up initially at Invermoriston at the mouth of Glenmoriston on the west side of Loch Ness, she opened a studio workshop, mainly wholesale, later transferring to Glen Urquhart, west of Drumnadrochit.

The premises at Beauly became available in 1994, and since then Lynda Usher Knitwear & Yarn, a homely, happy shop which is more of a gallery than a retail outlet, has specialized in providing top-of-the-range knitwear from small producers throughout the United Kingdom. In addition to her own creations, Lynda also retails an extensive range of yarns for hand knitters, an increasing rarity, and various items from small textile producers such as hand-dyed experimental works, and very individual felted hats. There is also an extension specializing in individual linen wear, skirts, pants, jackets and shirts.

Reflected in a mirror, Lynda Usher surveys the range of individually styled knitwear and (opposite) *the extensive range of yarns in her Highland shop.*

Gerald Laing
at Kinkell Castle

6 *A sculptor's workshop*

Gerald Laing at work on a maquette of a rugby lineout.

Opposite: *Apollo, specially commissioned, gazes in wonder at Kinkell Castle.*

It is thirty years since the sculptor Gerald Laing made his home on the Black Isle, north of Inverness. Having worked in both London and New York, he acquired the ruined Kinkell Castle, near Dingwall, in 1969, and courageously embarked upon an ambitious restoration programme.

Since then, the 16th-century keep, lovingly transformed into a comfortable and stylish home, has been his working base. In 1976, with the late George Mancine, he established his own bronze casting foundry exclusively to cast his own work. This was taken over in 1995 by Laing's son Farquhar, who now runs it as a commercial operation which he has re-named Black Isle Bronze, casting for his father as well as clients all over Britain.

All the rebuilding work at Kinkell was undertaken by Laing himself, and much to his delight he is constantly making new discoveries. For example, it has now emerged that all the dressed stone used for the windows, doors, corbels and fireplaces originated from Dundee, a distance of 180 miles in an age without roads. This suggests that the design and construction of the original castle was by a travelling group of masons who, given that the remainder of the building is fabricated from local rubble and whinstone, must have relied on their home quarry in Dundee for the more difficult stonework requirements. Laing's conclusion is supported by his discovery of a virtually identical building from the same period, but ruined down to the first floor, on the other side of the Cromarty Firth.

Kinkell is a very lucid, sophisticated and elegant piece of architecture. It has none of the design fudges, such as awkward changes of level, which are common in 16th-century building, so it is easy to imagine that the prototype of the period must have been popular.

Meanwhile, Gerald Laing's reputation as a sculptor remains international. In 1990 the insurance giant Standard Life commissioned *Axis Mundi*, a 25ft granite column with five 6ft-high bronze figures

Above: *Gerald Laing at work in his studio in the grounds of the castle.*

Right: *A bronze figure surveys the view over to Strathconnon.*

attached at the top, for its offices at Tanfield House in Edinburgh. The following year, the Federation of Master Builders approached him to create the Conan Doyle Memorial in Edinburgh, marking the site of Sir Arthur Conan Doyle's birthplace with a life-size sculpture of the author's greatest creation, Sherlock Holmes.

Laing's ouput is prodigious. In 1994 he made a portrait bust of Tam Dalyell MP commissioned by his wife Kathleen for The Binns, Dalyell's home near Edinburgh, with a copy for display at the Scottish National Portrait Gallery. In 1995 he created ten bronze dragons, each 6ft-high, for London's Bank Underground Station.

There followed four 9ft-high figures of rugby players for the stadium at Twickenham, commissioned by the Rugby Union; and the following year a portrait bust of Sir Paul Getty, KBE, which was commissioned by the National Gallery in London, led to Sir Paul's asking him to create a 14ft-high bronze of a cricketer for his cricket grounds in Buckinghamshire. Emphasizing his versatility, work recently completed includes ten glass panels, etched and inlaid, again for Standard Life's head office in Edinburgh.

Left *and* above: *The caryatid lamp fitting was designed by Gerald Laing, and there are many casts of it throughout Kinkell. There are many of his bronze portraits in the house; the two in the window are of his sons Farquhar and Clovis.*

Opposite: *The gilt gesso and mirrored processional cross dates from the 17th century. The doorway leads from the Great Hall to the main stairway.*

Kinkell Castle from the west.

Right: *Coat of arms of Ogilvie-Laing of Kinkell; and a sundial, the original commissioned by United Biscuits for Sir Hector Laing.*

Opposite: *A cast of the central figure in Laing's* Axis Mundi *bronze, commissioned by Standard Life in Edinburgh, overlooking the Boating Pond.*

7 *An architect's Highland retreat*

Ian Begg at work in his studio.

Opposite: *Ravens' Craig nestles in the steep slopes of the Wester Ross landscape.*

Tradition is a great teacher. That is what Ian Begg, one of Scotland's foremost architects, believes; it comprises the collective learning and experience of those who have gone before, stretching very far back into the past, and it comes right up to the present.

Qualifying as an architect in 1951, Ian began his working career with the Edinburgh-based firm headed up by Robert Hurd, a man who was to have a significant influence on Scotland's building design in the years that followed. The firm combined modern building work in the remoter parts of Scotland with an interest in the restoration of fine old buildings, something which especially appealed to the young architect, and which has remained a passion with him ever since. As the commissions came his way, he started to realize just how much Scotland was losing contact with its past.

By 1983, he had started a practice of his own, having landed two major projects which enabled him to express his deep feelings about the Scottish tradition in architecture. The first opportunity had come about when he was asked to create a medieval-style structure on the site of the demolished Bishop's Palace of Glasgow Cathedral. The second commission was for a modern hotel, which required him to reflect the adjacent vernacular architecture on Edinburgh's historic Royal Mile. Both projects earned him immediate acclaim.

By this stage, however, he had decided to create his own home. On several occasions he had been approached to renovate old tower houses, but had turned the offers down, deciding that it would be a far greater challenge for him to build his own, starting from scratch. When some land on the north-west coast, a region close to his heart, became available, it proved to be exactly what he had been looking for.

Ian's starting point was a great hall. Everything grew from that within as compact a floor plan as he could devise to accommodate the required rooms. A basic core contains the bulk of living space and the heating,

Left: *An alcove entrance into the dining hall.*

Right: *There is a faintly Gothic feel about the dining hall with its curved ceiling and arched doorways.*

the latter an essential requirement for living in a constantly changing and often chilly climate.

The total height of the house, from the ground outside to the ridge of the roof, is 17 metres. There are two stairways to gain access to the upper floors, one straight within the wall thickness, serving the master bedroom directly from the kitchen and great hall. The main stair is circular and turns anti-clockwise in its first and more elegant flight to the great hall, then reduces in scale, turning clockwise to serve the other bedrooms.

Ian looks back on the project as a brave adventure. Work started without his knowing if he would ever be able to make enough money to finish the job in a reasonable time. It was, he admits, a gamble. Today, with Ravens' Craig a feature on the wooded landscape and the Begg family happily installed, the gamble has paid off.

Above: *The Great Hall measures 5 x 7 metres. The decorative ceiling is based on equilateral triangles and the walls are covered with a slightly textured rough finish and painted.*

Right: *Ian Begg has created a delightful Italianate style loggia which enables him to enjoy spectacular views of the surrounding countryside. The main stair turns elegantly anti-clockwise in its flight from the Great Hall.*

The siting of Ravens' Craig means that it enjoys fine views over Loch Carron.

Roddy and Eric Langmuir
at Clach Mhor

8   *Designed for the family*

Eric Langmuir practises his mountaineering skills.

Opposite: *Natural materials abound in the interiors of Clach Mhor, a house that responds to the contours upon which it is sited.*

It says a great deal about this father and son relationship that when it came to building a house for himself, Eric Langmuir, a mountaineer with a great affection for the Highlands, should have turned to his son Roddy, a director of Edward Cullinan Architects, then in his early thirties.

The result was, of course, a very personal statement. The chosen site was a mere two miles from Scotland's winter sports mecca of Aviemore, and Roddy's grasp of his father's requirements was absolute. Tapered to mould into the generous landscape, the design is an example of non-confrontational modernism at its best, a Scandinavian-style retreat offering both views of the Cairngorm mountains and access to a much cherished landscape.

From a certain angle, the building looks like a caterpillar, from another as if a flying saucer has landed on the slopes above Avie Lochan, a bowl of bright water. The site occupies the southern half of a small knoll in the Spey Valley, left behind in the long ago glacial retreat.

To the south-east are views of the great arc of the Cairngorm mountains. A curved path leading from the roadway follows a natural rising bank and leads to the main door. Ten thousand years of Highland history are encapsulated in this landscape.

To begin with, Roddy worked on the designs in his own time, only calling it into the office once planning permission was granted in 1991. Building then began in earnest on the chosen site where an abundance of juniper was used to screen a parking area. The Langmuirs are pleased to announce that only one juniper bush was lost in the construction.

And following the same instincts, only natural materials were employed throughout: crystal-line glass and wood, rough sawn cedar, zinc, and render outside; plywood, white walls, concrete and timber floors inside. Exterior materials were chosen because of their ability to weather well and age gracefully. In time, the standing seam zinc roof will develop a deep blue-grey patina, and the cedar will silver with age.

The interior design creates a sense of spacious modern living. The steel ladder, a feature in itself, gives access to the roof.

Deep oversailing eaves shelter windows and wall heads from weather, and planted walls of boulders, masonry and slate protect the outdoor terraces. The low pitch roof, and a building section which creates three levels of cut from the bank, combine to adapt the house to the contours upon which its sits.

So the basement, dining terrace, bedroom terrace, and the long north-western elevation where the ground is at sill level, could each be said to interact in a deliberate way with the natural surroundings. Both Eric and

Roddy agree that the house is a stage to the drama of Highland weather. Internally, however, the rooms are all gathered to maximize the feeling of generosity of space. Bathrooms and bedrooms occupy the north-east end of the house and sleeping platforms make use of the extra height of the ridge in the tradition of the mountain bothy.

Downstairs is the 'wet' entrance, sheltered by the bay window and eaves above, propped from a 40-ton granite boulder, the Clach Mhor ('Big Stone' in Gaelic) from which the house takes its name. A circular sauna is a warm heart beneath the dining platform above.

The fortunes of Aviemore as a Highland playground began when the railway arrived on the way to Inverness in the 1880s. Almost 100 years later the Aviemore Centre was built, and facilities to cater for the

Above left: *A ladder and submarine-like access are provided to a roof turret.*

Above: *The windows and walls are protected from extremes of weather by the overhanging eaves.*

increasingly popular pastimes of skiing in the winter and mountaineering in the summer, were developed to attract significant numbers of visitors to the region.

Today the area and its facilities are constantly upgraded to offer a choice of hotels, shops and a major swimming pool and ice-rink complex, but there is still more than enough open space available in the surrounding wilderness-countryside to cater for the army of hillwalkers and bird watchers who use it as an exploration base throughout the year. The joys of living in Speyside are plentiful, not least because it is possible to have the best of two worlds: the convenience of a well-constructed community life near at hand, and the opportunity for instant escape into the mountains, sweeping birch woods, drowned land, and open skies, unspoiled by human kind.

All this was very much in the minds of both father and son when they embarked upon their project. A beacon in the landscape and a cherished retreat, Clach Mhor both complements and enhances the environment in which it sits.

The shape and structure of the building were dictated by the desire to fit it into the natural existing landscape.
Above: *Eric Langmuir inspects the standing seam zinc roof which will eventually develop a coloured patina. In time the cedar struts will silver.*

Designed for the family 79

Susannah Stone
at Knockbreck House

9 *A gourmet legacy*

Susannah Stone and 'Bite' welcome visitors.

Opposite: *The hall, with its elegant staircase and 'the happiest of atmospheres'.*

Like so many individual success stories, the enterprise began almost by accident. For years Susannah Stone, a farmer's wife in Easter Ross, had been making cheese in the bathtub for her husband Reggie and sons, Ruariadh and James.

During one such cheese-making session, back in 1962, she misjudged the quantity required for a weekly supply for family and friends, and decided on the spur of the moment to take the excess to Hector Ross, her local grocer in Tain. Hector was only too delighted to accept it in lieu of unpaid grocery bills, and almost overnight there was a demand. Susannah's Caboc double fresh cream cheese rolled in toasted pinhead oatmeal became a much sought-after gourmet item, and within months she was not only making it, but delivering bulk supplies on the farm tractor to keep up with the orders.

Caboc was a family recipe, said to have originated from the Western Isles in the 16th century, and passed down to Susannah from her ancestor Mariota d'Ile, a daughter of the Clan Donald Lord of the Isles. 'Certainly it was being used by my great-grandmother and passed on,' she says. On a visit to the island of Islay, once the stronghold of Clan Donald, she was told of how, when Campbells came to kidnap Mariota, then an infant, her mother had hid her in the barrel in which she made Caboc.

Knockbreck, which has been Susannah's home since 1956, was originally built for the long-established Highland family of Ross in the 17th century, the construction semi-fortified as was the custom and necessity of the age. Some of the original lintels can still be seen on the back wall, where two 200-year-old beech trees encroach upon the stonework. The high wall to the rear once extended around the parkland.

In 1737, it is recorded that David Ross of Invercarron took possession of the Old Manor, as it was then called, from Robert Ross of Achnacloich. He immediately set about renovating the building, removing doors, creating access through the windows, and generally restructuring the

Top: *Ardbreck House, largely rebuilt in the late 18th century with Tain sandstone.*
Above: *The assembly line for Cabok cheese at Highland Fine Cheeses.*

Opposite: *A tester bed in a comfortable guest bedroom.*

interiors. In addition, he is accused of 'embezzling and conveying away 200 standard arms (muskets).' Two centuries later, W. Macgill, author of *Old Ross-shire and Scotland as seen in the Tain and Balnagowan documents,* records that contemporaries were unimpressed. One of them even went so far as to observe that 'When he got possession, it was watertight. Now a great deal of the roof is without thatch and the bottle racks broken.'

In 1790, the property was acquired by the Baillie family and largely rebuilt, using the remarkably smart sandstone from the Tain quarry. Thereafter, it was occupied by various Rosses and Macdonalds, and eventually, during the 20th century, sold to Sandy Smith, a sculptor. Following the death of her mother in 1954, Susannah's father decided to move to Easter Ross to live with his daughter and son-in-law, and it was then that Reggie Stone had an inspiration.

Sandy Smith, their neighbour, who was also a family friend, had been spending increasingly more time in London, and Knockbreck was uninhabited for long periods in the year. Reggie paid Sandy and his wife a visit to ask if they might be interested in selling. They agreed.

'It was a dreary February day when we went to look it over,' recalls Susannah. 'The hall was dark green and rather gloomy, but I remember thinking that it had the happiest atmosphere.you could imagine.'

And within months she found herself living there and bringing up her two sons. The atmosphere has never changed.

In 1963, she and Reggie gave up farming and converted their cow byre into a cheese factory. Highland Fine Cheeses was officially launched and, as a family company run by Ruariadh Stone, currently employs twelve cheesemakers and produces a range of full, medium and low fat cheese products which are sent all over the world. James Stone, a director, has skilfully negotiated the upgrading of factory facilities necessary to meet European Community requirements, and Susannah, having little regard for feminist political correctness, is officially designated Chairman, although she prefers to be called The Founder. Today she shares Knockbreck with James and his wife and young family.

Suki Urquhart at Old Mayens

10 *A Banffshire garden*

Suki Urquhart at work in her studio.

Opposite: *The terraced gardens with views to the south towards the River Deverom.*

While the poor soil and the abundance of natural predators such as rabbit and deer have never made it easy for the great gardens of the Highlands to survive, where somebody takes an interest and is prepared to work hard at it, the results can be spectacular. Sir Islay Campbell of Succoth's Crarae gardens in Argyll and the superb National Trust for Scotland gardens at Inverewe spring readily to mind; also the walled garden created by the Queen Mother at the Castle of Mey in Caithness.

Suki Urquhart, a landscape gardener who has recently found the recognition she deserves, with regular gardening columns and a series of television features, discovered this one-acre garden on the edge of Banffshire when it was little more than a run-down field. The 17th-century house that it surrounded, part of a larger estate with a Georgian mansion as the principal residence, was in poor repair. Sadly neglected, a few ancient trees had survived the howling gales that sweep with predictable regularity up the glen, and the original carriage drive had become a tractor road. A proportion of the front entrance area was employed as a farm mechanic's pit.

Suki, with an imaginative and experienced eye, instantly saw the potential. A large digger took ten days to alter the uneasy continuous slope upon which the house was perched into inter-connecting terraces to afford protection from the wind. At the same time she opened up stunning views of the distant river and the amphitheatre of surrounding hills.

Completely overgrown, with scented honeysuckles and roses, the garden remains hidden from the approaching road, affording a complete sensation of privacy. A small summerhouse at the edge of the garden sits 200 yards above the river and leads the eye across countryside which has remained unchanged for centuries. The mechanic's pit area has been walled and paved and now supports a mixture of herbs and cottage garden plants. The walls are covered with rambling roses, climbers and

espaliered fruit trees. Through a rustic gate, a small triangular area bordered by mixed herbs contains annual herbs, herbaceous plants, salads and nursery beds. This leads off into an ordered vegetable garden growing soft fruit, potatoes and other annual vegetables.

But when you pass through the archway in the beech hedge, the mood alters. Green lawns linked by grass paths tumble down the hillside surrounded and intersected with borders. Mixed plantains, nearly 100 different species, are closely underplanted with herbaceous plants, creeping ground cover and smaller shrubs.

As an example of Suki's inventiveness, a small stone pond in the centre of the lawn has its raised walls planted with alpines, its inside with a white scented lily, while a bronze fish lazily acts as a fountain. An arch of pollarded red limes leads to a path along a diagonal bed filled with golden plants and a few scattered trees with golden honeysuckle growing through them. Protecting this border from the prevailing south-west wind is a mixed hedge of larch and rugosa roses where verbascum and white foxglove have established themselves as if by accident.

To those in the know, it is obvious that such gardens do not happen by chance, even if they give the appearance of having done so. That is the great secret. A glorious garden must always look as if it has come together through the accident of time.

Suki's landscape gardening work now takes her all over Scotland and beyond. She has recently been commissioned to work in Spain, designing a swimming pool and its surrounding terraces. 'It doesn't really matter where you are, the design has to complement the house and sit comfortably within the surrounding landscape,' she says. 'Thus the colours, patterns and textures of the plants, stones and buildings should merge as though they were all part of the same tapestry.'

Above: *Mixed planting in front of the Witch's Turret.*
Right: *Mecanopsis (Blue Himalayan Poppy).*

Above top: *The courtyard showing the Hackett and Abernethy coat of arms dating from the 17th century.*
Above: *Tea in the courtyard.*
Right: *The 19th-century wing seen from the fish pond.*

The Front Hall with a mirror decorated with shells which Suki collected in the Western Isles.

Below: *Scottish sponge ware on the kitchen dresser with decorated eggs.*

Right: *The sitting room, a model of cosiness and comfort.*

The front entrance of Old Mayens
with yellow and grey Mediterranean-
style planting.

11 *Guarding the Sound of Mull*

Sir Lachlan Maclean on the clifftop of Duart.

Opposite: *The Banqueting Hall. The flags are the regimental colours of the 236th Battalion, Canadian Expeditionary Force, The Maclean Kilties of America. The fireplace incorporates Sir Lachlan's coat of arms as 28th Chief of Clan Maclean.*

In February 1979, John Dadd, a naval diving instructor, exploring the shelf of water in the bay below Duart Castle, discovered an iron cannon and an anchor. He kept his secret for twelve years before contacting the archaeological unit at St Andrews University. And then the search was on.

Duart Castle, the ancient fortress of Clan Maclean, has been under attack many times since its oldest walls were erected in the mid-13th century. The location for the fortification was well chosen, sited on a high crag at the end of a peninsula, *Dubh Ard* in Gaelic, meaning 'Black Point', which juts out into the Sound of Mull to command the channel between the island of Mull, the mainland, including the entrances of Lochs Linnhe and Etive, and the neck of the Firth of Lorne.

Long ago Norse and Viking warships relentlessly raided this coastline, taking no captives. The Macleans of Duart formed a loose alliance with the other west-coast Scotland chiefs to lend support to the Clan Donald Lord of the Isles, who operated a chain of eight castles on each side of the Sound, all within sight of each other. Thus a beacon signal could be instantly transmitted from Mingary Castle on Ardnamurchan Point, opposite Duart, via six others, including Duart, to Dunollie Castle, close to Oban, to warn of approaching danger.

Times were tough and violent in that bygone age, and Duart Castle, with walls varying between 3 to 7 metres in thickness, has seen more than its share of bloodshed. But the cannon discovered in Duart Bay originates from a much later century, marking a watershed in the fortunes of this island clan.

The power and influence of Clan Maclean in the Hebrides had reached its zenith during and following the Spanish Armada of 1588, when the then chief, Sir Lachlan Mor, while owing allegiance to the King of Scots, had secretly treated with not only Queen Elizabeth I of England, but also the Spanish invaders.

Top: *The carved stone of Lord Maclean's coat of arms is above the main entrance to the castle. It was presented by his clansfolk in 1986 to commemorate his fifty years as chief.*

Above: *A mock-up of a Victorian maid's pantry sunk deep into the castle walls.*

However, at the same time on the mainland, Clan Campbell was fast growing in strength, hungry for land, and gaining influence at the Stuart Court. Not surprisingly, James VI of Scotland, who became King of England in 1603, took a dim view of the Macleans' double dealing and took steps to sequester Duart to the King's Commissioners, though allowing the family to remain.

And no doubt because of this, the Macleans did remain loyal to the House of Stuart throughout the ensuing Civil War, Sir Hector Ruadh Maclean being killed at the Battle of Inverkeithing in 1651, with eight of his foster brothers and 500 of his clansmen.

Two years thereafter, Oliver Cromwell, declared Protector by the English Parliament in the same year, sent ships to destroy Duart, but when they arrived they found the castle empty. Before they could do much else, however, a great north-westerly gale blew up which lasted for seventeen hours and sank three of the ships, and it is the artefacts from these ships – sword hilts, pots, and buckles – which are currently being salvaged from the bay under the supervision of the Scottish Institute of Maritime Studies.

In the aftermath of all this, the Macleans, having mortgaged the greater proportion of their lands, found themselves deeply in debt, their loans being largely bought up by the Campbells. Thus the confrontations between the Macleans and the Campbells continued, and when Sir John Maclean of Duart in 1689 led his clansmen in support of the Jacobite cause at the Battle of Killiecrankie, it gave the Campbells just the excuse they were looking for.

Following the ensuing Jacobite defeat, they deployed 2,500 men to scatter the Macleans and drive them from their homeland. Until 1751, Duart Castle was used as a garrison for government troops, and over a century and a half was to pass before Colonel Sir Fitzroy Maclean, 26th Chief, having been taken to see the ruin as a boy, remarked, 'It is going to be my life's ambition to restore the castle as a family home, and as headqarters of the clan.'

In 1911, at the age of 76, he began the work of restoration, a monumental task given that by then most of the roof had disappeared and the walls were crumbling. When he reached the age of 100, he received a telegram from the Duke of Argyll suggesting that on such an auspicious

occasion the feud with the Campbells should end. Maclean replied, 'Certainly, for my lifetime!'

Today Duart Castle, gaunt and austere on its clifftop vantage point, is the home of Sir Fitzroy's grandson, Sir Lachlan Maclean, 28th Chief, who with his wife Mary, two sons and daughter continues to honour the family traditions. Duart Castle is open to the public from April until October, a magnet to the thousands of Macleans scattered throughout the world, and Sir Lachlan, a former officer in the Scots Guards, is only too happy to welcome them back to their ancestral home.

In the meantime, the underwater searches continue on a seasonal basis, bringing together a constant flow of new information about a bygone age, a fascinating insight into the confrontational politics of Scotland four hundred years ago.

Duart Castle with saltire flag flapping in the wind, seen from the landward side. The clifftop dominates the Sound of Mull.

Duart Castle stands like a looming sentinel guarding the waterways between the island of Mull, mainland Scotland and the neck of the Firth of Lorne. It was in these waters that ships sent by Oliver Cromwell to subdue the Clan Maclean in 1653 sank in a storm and twenty-seven sailors were drowned. A collection of items recently retrieved by divers can be seen in the castle.

12 *Model railway to a sculpture garden*

*Christopher James on the Statue Walk
at Torosay Castle.*

Opposite: *The Castle from the south.
The Top Terrace drops down steps
onto the Fountain Terrace, two of the
three Italianate terraces created by the
distinguished Scottish architect Sir
Robert Lorimer.*

On the even hours, large car-ferries depart from the bay of the west-coast mainland town of Oban for the island of Mull, returning at odd hours. A stone's throw from the ferry landing at Craignure, their first port of call, is the Old Pier Station where a succession of steam and diesel hauled trains stand by to transport passengers to and from Torosay Castle and Gardens, one of the island's main tourist attractions.

David Guthrie-James and his mother Bridget inherited Torosay Castle in 1945, and although they briefly allowed it to become a hotel called *The Tangle of the Isles*, by 1972 it was decided that the family had the option of either letting it fall into decay, or to restore it and share its charm with others. It was David who, with a railway enthusiast neighbour, came up with the idea of building the little 10-inch narrow-gauge railway, a mile and a half long. Today magnificent Torosay Castle, with its spectacular gardens and Statue Walk, is the home of David's son Christopher, who has steadily restored and enhanced the property, and continues to open it to the public from April until mid-October. The gardens remain open throughout daylight hours the year round.

David Guthrie-James was an intriguing character who wrote *Escaper's Progress*, an enthralling account of his escape from a German prisoner-of-war camp, and who served as Member of Parliament for Brighton Kemp Town, and then North Dorset. As a young man he rounded the Horn as a deck-hand in *Viking*, one of the last of the purely commercial Finnish four-masted barques, and towards the end of his life dedicated much of his time to attempting to prove the existence of the Loch Ness Monster.

In 1950, he married Jacquetta Digby, daughter of 11th Baron Digby and younger sister of the late Pamela Harriman, former wife of Randolph Churchill, who was the United States Ambassador to France at the time of her death in 1997. The scrapbooks in the Archive Room, filled with newspaper cuttings about the family collected over nearly a century, can monopolize an entire visit.

Originally, there was a much smaller Georgian house where Torosay Castle now stands, but this was demolished in 1850 by its owner John Campbell to build Duart House. The eminent architect David Bryce was contracted to create a home in the Scottish baronial style, but it appears that the ultimate cost involved was too much for Campbell, who was obliged to sell the estate in 1865.

The purchaser was Arbuthnot Charles Guthrie, the prosperous younger son of the co-founder of a small merchant bank called Chalmers Guthrie of Dundee and London. He was Christopher James's great-great-great uncle, and it was his nephew and immediate heir, Murray Guthrie, who enlisted the help of Sir Robert Lorimer, the great Edwardian architect, to create the three Italianate terraces and the Statue Walk which connect the Castle and the old Walled Garden.

Within the twelve acres of garden are roses and other climbers, underplanted with perennials. Steps down into the gardens are flanked by marble urns filled with echevarias, leading to a circular lawn featuring a marble statue of Artemesia surrounded by berberis, potentillas, and junipers. A further flight of steps leads to the Statue Walk, where there are nineteen lifesize limestone figures created by Antonio Bonazza (1698-1763).

Above *and* Opposite: *Life-size figures by Antonio Bonazza acquired in northern Italy by Murray Guthrie. The Fountain Terrace commands a spectacular view across the Bay towards Duart Castle.*

Right: *The Mull Railway which runs along 1½ miles of narrow-gauge track transporting visitors between Torosay Castle and the ferry teminal at Craignure.*

Murray Guthrie acquired this remarkable collection from a deserted villa near Padua in northern Italy, and brought them to Torosay at the turn of the century, using them as ballast for his boat. The figures represent gardeners, gamekeepers, fishermen and women and are set against a hedge of Fuchsia magellanica which grows at their feet.

Murray died in 1911, but shortly before his death sold the ruins of Duart Castle, which sat upon his estate, to Sir Fitzroy Maclean, the 77-year-old Chief of Clan Maclean. At the same time he agreed to re-name his home Torosay, after the pre-Reformation name of the parish in which it stands, and which in the Gaelic, loosely translated, means 'a hill covered with shrubs.'

Today the two properties, in sight of one another across Duart Bay, are almost complementary. A visit to one invariably means a visit to the other, and an opportunity to reflect upon the ancient, warfaring days of

The Guthrie children painted in 1903 by Frederick Whiting RP, showing David (12), Violet (10), Bridget (15), and Patrick (18).

the islands and the Victorian prosperity which followed the industrial revolution of the 19th century.

Aside from opening the Castle to the public, Christopher James is a farmer, owning a herd of pedigree Highland cattle. He and his wife Sarah have a daughter Fenella, and Torosay Castle is managed on a highly professional basis with a tearoom offering home baking, and a gift shop selling local produce.

Above left: *An alcove window overlooking the Lion Terrace.*
Left: *View from the Drawing Room window onto the Italianate terraces.*
Above: *Antlers of red deer stags overlook the entrance and front hall-*
way. The tiger was shot by the present owner's grandmother in 1922.
Years later she went on a camera safari and said that she felt ashamed
of herself for having killed such a fine animal.

Model railway to a sculpture garden 103

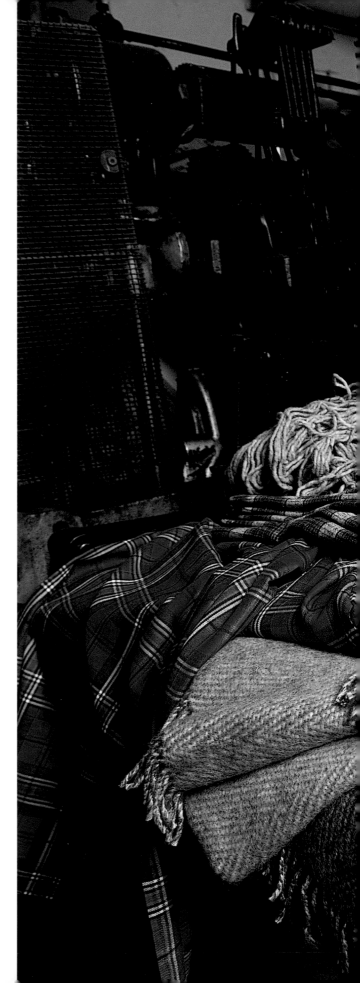

Bob Ryan at work with one of his dobby looms. Right: *Kathy Ryan supervises the sorting of rugs and woollen items, brightly coloured tartans and stylish weaves.*

Isle of Mull weavers

It is twelve years since Bob and Kathy Ryan first approached Christopher James about creating a workshop to manufacture tweed, travel and floor rugs, scarves, and various other woollen items. Premises in some old farm steadings were made available at the end of a little lane, off the front drive to the castle. Having introduced traditional weaving on old dobby looms dating from 1924 and 1958, Isle of Mull Weavers is now a major cottage industry.

An amiable English couple who have intergrated effortlessly into the local community, Bob demonstrates the weaving to anybody who shows an interest and Kathy runs the shop. Whatever they make is never repeated, but nevertheless their output, featuring both subtle and brighly coloured wools and threads, is today much in demand all over the world.

Andrew and Nicola Bradford
at Kincardine Castle

13   *A sporting estate*

SEASONS FOR GAME SPORT

Red & Sika Stags *July-Oct*
Roe buck *Apr-Oct*
Fallow buck *Aug-Apr*
Red & Sika hinds/Hybrids *Oct-Feb*
Fallow doe *Oct-Mar*
Roe doe *Oct-Mar*
Grouse *Aug-Oct*
Partridge *Sep-Feb*
Pheasant *Oct-Feb*
Salmon *Jan-Oct*
Trout *Mar-Oct*
Rainbow Trout *Any time*

Opposite: *The oak panelled Great Hall.*

Autumn days spent in the heather with a gun and a dog raising the grouse or skirting the woodlands for pheasant, soft spring evenings on the river casting for salmon, and fresh, windswept walks on the high ground stalking the deer...

As the night closes in, friends gather under the stags' antlers in the Great Hall to dine off the game, fish and venison freshly caught, and to toast your health in a single malt distilled in the nearby distillery. This is the fabled Scotland which in the mid-19th century inspired Queen Victoria and her German husband Prince Albert to purchase their beloved Balmoral Castle in the Deeside forests of Aberdeenshire. The scenery reminded Albert of his homeland Thuringerwald and he took to the sporting traditions of the Highland way of life in such a manner that before long all of British high society was following his example.

Under rich patronage, the sporting estates of the north of Scotland have continued to make a significant contribution to the rural economy, but often at the expense of the owner. Towards the end of the millennium, however, there has been a more commercial and modern emphasis placed on land management, and sporting estates are now expected to pay their way.

Andrew and Nicola Bradford inherited the Kincardine Estate from Andrew's mother in 1984, and although it is now commercially let on an occasional basis, it remains very much their home where, to a very great extent, they continue to carry on the traditions his family have maintained for a hundred years.

Built in 1894, Kincardine was designed, like so many Victorian country houses of the day, as an entertainment machine. As a whimsical footnote, the architects responsible, David Niven and his brother-in-law Herbert Wigglesworth, went on that same year to design the luxury saloon for the SS *Tantallon Castle* of the famous Union Castle Line. In the early years, the sumptuousness of the interiors were often compared, but since the

Left: *The entrance hall with a stained glass window above a mirror and chest flanked by footmen's chairs.* Above: *A long view of the Great Hall where the Bradfords frequently hold musical evenings for family and friends.* Right: *An old notice itemizing the rods and reels in the fishing cupboard.* Top right: *Andrew and Nicola Bradford entertaining a shooting party to lunch.*

SS *Tantallon Castle* now lies at the bottom of the sea, it is hard to judge. Large and comfortable, nevertheless, Kincardine was always intended as a base for family and friends to enjoy the distractions of the sporting playground of Deeside. It therefore clearly made sense for Andrew and Nicola, when they took on the responsibilities of the estate, to make it available to others on a commercial basis, not only for shooting and fishing parties, but also for business meetings, residential seminars and small conferences.

Set in 3,000 acres of hilly, wooded countryside, and with over three miles of the north bank of the River Dee on the estate, Kincardine offers the full range of country sports from clay and game shoots to fly-only salmon fishing. Activities not available on the estate itself, such as stalking, golf and gliding, can all be arranged in the immediate vicinity.

And with Inverness 100 miles to the west, Aberdeen 25 miles northeast, and Edinburgh 120 miles to the south, Kincardine, close to the village of Kincardine O'Neill and Aboyne, is extraordinarily well located.

Approached up a long drive, the house takes privacy for granted. Within an hour's drive from Aberdeen Airport, guests can escape into all the comforts of a well-established Highland lifestyle.

Thus while shooting parties enjoy driven pheasants followed by lunch in Kincardine's grand dining room, others come to stay simply for the

A sporting estate 109

Above: *Casting for salmon on the River Dee.*

Opposite: *A morning's pheasant shoot in the woods.*

spectacular location and peace and quiet which Kincardine offers. Moreover, as it is their home, the Bradfords are on hand as host and hostess, organizing the staff and outside suppliers to meet requirements, and choosing the food and wines for the entertainment. Both are talented musicians and have their own Scottish country dance band. Often after dinner, the entire household will gather around the piano for an old-fashioned evening of musical entertainment.

Turret windows and water spouts for drainage.

Right: *Kincardine Castle loftily surveys the surrounding forests and sweeping landscape of Kincardine O'Neill, looking south-west across Deeside towards Balmoral and Lochnagar.*

Douglas and Mary Lindsay on the yacht *Corryvreckan*

14 *All at sea*

Douglas and Mary Lindsay revel in the fresh air and freedom afforded by the yachting life.

Opposite: *The yacht* Corryvreckan *sets sail into the Hebrides.*

The Hebrides, the necklace of islands off the west of Scotland, is the stuff of which dreams are made. And it was a dream shared by Douglas and Mary Lindsay when they launched their yacht charter venture over thirty years ago.

Pure white beaches, the legendary Fingal's Cave on the isle of Staffa, the gardens of Inverewe on the mainland and on offshore Gigha, all are within reach. A trip to the Christian monastery on Iona, to Canna and St Kilda, the nearest landmass to the Americas, with sightings of seals, dolphins and whales, anything is possible with the yacht *Corryvreckan*.

Born and brought up close to Edinburgh, Douglas was drawn to the sea from childhood. Mary, whose family home was in Argyll, had reservations to begin with. They married in 1968, and bought their first boat the following year. The business prospered, but during the 1970s there was an interlude while their two children were growing up. In 1980, however, they were back on the high seas with the first *Corryvreckan*.

Built in 1990 to a high specification especially for holiday cruises on the West Coast of Scotland, the second *Corryvreckan* is described by Douglas and Mary as 'big, blue and beautiful'. For over ten seasons, she has been their home, providing their guests with comfort and safety, and superlative catering.

For there is nothing Mary enjoys more than cooking in the galley, to such a standard that she has been nominated a member of Taste of Scotland, the Scottish Tourist Board-backed scheme which promotes Scotland's natural larder.

Operating out of the town of Oban, *Corryvreckan* is equipped for long-distance sailing and has crossed the Atlantic four times with a good turn of speed. Although a big modern yacht, her Bermudan ketch rig means that her large sail area is split up into units more easily handled by the crew. Below decks there is full headroom throughout, and with a high standard of insulation and central heating the accommodation is kept

warm and dry whatever the weather outside. The five two-berth guest cabins all have comfortable full-sized bunks equipped with cosy continental quilts and there are plenty of hatches and portholes to keep them bright and airy. The three toilet compartments all have wash basins and efficient showers with plenty of hot water.

In the spacious saloon there is comfortable seating on both sides of the boat and a dining table large enough to seat twelve. A library includes reference books on Scotland, wildlife and sailing, and a selection of games and tapes is provided for those nights anchored far from the nearest civilization.

In the deckhouse, which houses the chart table and navigation instruments, there is space to sit and enjoy the scenery without being exposed to the wind and weather, always unpredictable in the Hebrides where

Corryvreckan *anchored off the island of Staffa, which incorporates the legendary Fingal's Cave.*
Left: *Sailing gear and Ship's Orders.*

Opposite above: *Mary Lindsay shows what the crew will have for dinner.*
Right: *The spacious saloon provides an excellent library for holiday reading and comfortable seating on both sides.*

there is an old saying that you can experience all the seasons of a year in one day. In fact, the rainfall is lower in Scotland's Western Isles than in the Highlands, but the changeability of the climate and the constantly moving light on the land and the water are what gives this seascape its extraordinary allure.

It may be offputting for some, but those who sign on for an adventure on the *Corryvreckan* are there to learn the sailor's craft. As members of the crew they are expected to want to learn about steering, navigation, hauling the ropes and stowing the sails, but all in good spirit. Under Douglas's watchful eye, everybody learns how to hoist and set the sails, to tie the necessary knots and keep everything shipshape on board, with the skipper happy to enlighten those who want to know more about navigation and seamanship.

At the end of a day's sailing there is time for exercise and exploration ashore, followed by Mary's spectacular cooking. Each night is spent in a safe anchorage, either peaceful or remote, sometimes near a small town with pubs and people. There is nowhere along this coastline that is unfamiliar to this enthusiastic and engaging couple who genuinely have succeeded in making their dream come true.

Mike Taitt
and his railway carriage

15 *Off track*

Mike Taitt and Archie, the labrador, beside the swimming pond.

Opposite: *A tartan bedspread covers the splendid brass bedstead. The carriage windows afford fine views across the surrounding countryside.*

Brought up on a farm near Craigellachie, in Banffshire, Major Mike Taitt served as a regular army officer with the Gordon Highlanders for twenty years before returning to the land and a farmhouse on the northern slopes of Bennachie, in Aberdeenshire. A confirmed bachelor, he has made a career out of restoring historic buildings, and lives an active life as an elder of the kirk, a justice of the peace, a voluntary case worker for the Architectural Heritage Society, and a committee member for the Scottish Game Conservancy. He is also wonderfully talented with his hands, and there is nothing he enjoys more than the challenge of fixing things himself.

A hearty out-of-doors character, Mike likes to swim during the summer months regardless of the weather, and to this end he has created a swimming pool for himself in a field below his farm. The problem to begin with was that there was nowhere for him to change and sit. That was soon put right when a neighbour announced the sale of a 1908 third-class North East Railway Company passenger carriage, which was being used as a hen house. Mike immediately offered him £100.

The neighbour had bought the carriage from the Inverurie Locomotive Works during the 1950s when the Great Northern Scottish Railway Company sold its rolling stock. Within days it was transferred to Mike's field, and within months a bow window extension and a balcony sitting area had been added.

Today the railway carriage has become almost a second home for Mike and his friends, fully equipped with domestic comforts. Calor gas lamps have been fitted and antique gas bracket lights that would only work on town gas have had brass ashtrays welded onto them to take candles instead.

Materials used for the restoration have almost all been recycled and have cost virtually nothing: for instance, tiles from a kitchen knocked down in the village. An 'umbrella tree', shading the carriage, has been

Above: *Mike has furnished his hide-away in a practical and elegant style.* Right below: *With a flick of this heat regulator, the draught hatch on the stove lights up.* Opposite: *A stylish retreat on the slopes of Bennachie.*

made from two metal cupola covers thrown out after the restoration of a local castle roof.

Mike Taitt says there is nowhere else in the world he would prefer to live. Even though he loves to travel, the carriage provides a real retreat from the demands of 20th-century living, enabling him to read and relax and listen to the classical music he loves, particularly during the long winter evenings.

Tony and Jean Gardner
at Ploughman's Hall

16 *An ideal conversion*

Tony and Jean Gardner with Jean's home baking.

Opposite: *Ploughman's Hall, extensively renovated and brought back to life again.*

It was love at first sight when Tony and Jean Gardner came across the Ploughman's Hall at Old Rayne, a picturesque little village on the River Ury, north-west of Aberdeen. Having lived for many years abroad, it was primarily Jean, originally from Skene, a small town some ten miles to the south of Old Rayne, who influenced the couple's decision to settle in Aberdeenshire.

'Having spent most of her life being where I wanted to be, I thought it about time I spent some time where she wanted to be,' says Tony. But when the couple first saw the building in 1984, they both recognized its potential. It was being used as a hay barn at the time, but had obviously known better days.

And so it had, for on further investigation Tony discovered that it had been built in 1820 as the only meeting hall of the Freefield Ploughman's Society. To this day there remains on the south wall a coat of arms carrying the insignia of the Ploughman's Society alongside those of the Leiths of Freefield, the landowning Aberdeenshire family who held the local barony and who no doubt contributed to the cost.

When the Freefield Ploughman's Society wound up in 1875, their headquarters became a croft and pub until 1910, after which it was converted into upper and lower floor flat accommodation and occupied by various owners until the 1950s. Thereafter it fell into disrepair and was used as a barn until Tony and Jean decided to rescue it.

But it was far from an easy conversion. The Gardners bought the property in 1985, but since it was in such a poor state they were obliged to gut the interior completely. Then the roof had to be replaced. Since there was only an outside staircase, an interior one had to be installed, but at the same time everything needed to comply with the regulations governing an historic B-Listed building.

Nevertheless, the Gardners were also determined to restore as far as possible the original intention, but for modern, practical living.

The entire top floor, once the meeting hall of the Freefield Ploughman's Society, has been transformed into a large, spacious living room.

Left: *A full-size family bake.*

Below: *Herbs from the garden hung out to dry.*

Right: *A coat of arms with the insignia of the Ploughman's Society alongside the Leiths of Freefield is carved into the south wall.*

For example, the entire top floor, which had served as the meeting hall, looks much as it would have done when it was first built, but is now their living room. The ground floor, which would have been used for storage, has been fitted with three bedrooms and a carpentry workshop for Tony.

Purchasing part of the adjoining field, they have transformed this into a glorious garden, and in 1995, not surprisingly, Ploughman's Hall won the Gordon District Conservation Award for house and garden, a welcome recognition for what can be done with a bit of imagination, not to mention determination.

Since then, in 1997, and with the help of Mike Taitt whose railway carriage also features in this book, Tony and Jean have restored the old byre in the grounds as a general utility store and overflow accommodation for friends and relatives who come to stay during the summer months.

17   *The monks of Pluscarden*

*A monk plays the pump organ which
was manufactured in Carnoustie
in 1884.*

Opposite: *Solitude and silence on a
warm summer's day.*

It was David I of Scotland, youngest son of the sainted Queen Margaret, who, in order to rule Scotland, set up a series of abbeys throughout his realm to act essentially as listening posts. The Highlands in the first millennium were as remote from the centre of power as it was possible to be, so these religious outposts, acting with missionary zeal to combat the remnants of Druidism, proved invaluable.

David's successors followed his example, and it was his great-grandson Alexander II who in 1230 founded a Valliscaulian priory at Pluscarden, south-west of Elgin on the Moray Firth. Two centuries later, this order joined forces with Urquhart, another Morayshire priory of the Benedictine persuasion founded by David I, and both became a dependency of the Benedictine monks of Dunfermline Abbey, brought to Scotland from Cambridge by Queen Margaret around 1070.

Needless to say, because of the nature of their job and the influence they wielded, Scotland's abbeys found themselves with a tough role to play over the centuries, often coming under attack from friend and foe alike. In 1389, for example, Alexander Stewart, who was appointed Lieutenant of the North by his brother Robert III, and whose ferocity earned him the title of the Wolf of Badenoch, torched Pluscarden during a personal feud with the Bishops of Moray and Ross.

But Pluscarden rose again, and certainly enjoyed a period of prosperity up until the Reformation in the 16th century. Settled upon the Seton family who became earls of Dunfermline, it rapidly became redundant, although monks continued in evidence for a few years. But after that, the estate was bought and sold among various local landowners, and the abbey, being only periodically used by Free Kirk, inevitably fell into disrepair.

It was to be almost two hundred years before salvation arrived. The 3rd Marquess of Bute, a convert to Catholicism, was a great antiquarian, and when its plight was brought to his attention in 1897, he immediately

set out to rebuild Pluscarden. However, as he had many other concerns, it took a long time, and the work was slowly continued after his death by his son Lord Colum Crichton Stuart, who eventually made the estate over to Prinknash Abbey in Gloucester.

The restoration continued, and in 1948 the priory was sufficiently advanced for the monks to move back in. With independence granted in 1966, Pluscarden was elevated to the status of Abbey in 1974. Today it houses twenty-seven monks who have given up all worldly goods and possessions. Following the rules set out for the monastic order by St Benedict, which dates from 1,500 years ago, it is only spiritual possessions that count in this life and the next.

But that does not exclude all contact with the outside world. At Pluscarden there is a guest wing where both men and women regularly come to stay for retreats, take part in the worship and talk to each other, but they are bound by the rules of silence which apply to any of the activities they share with the monks.

Every day the monks rise at 4.30 a.m. for their devotions, before going about their daily tasks in silence. The gardens are neatly tended, and food is grown for the kitchen. Bees are kept for honey, beeswax and Benet's Balm. The staple diet is fish and vegetables. Meat is served only at Sunday lunch and to the sick.

Opposite: *Candles are lit by Father Giles in the Chapel.*

Above left: *Brother Drostan pours water in the refectory.*

Above: *The monks' cowls hang outside the entrance to the cloisters. The cloth from which they are made is woven locally by Hugh Jones at Knockando Woollen Mill.*

Brother Cyprian is working on a stained glass window project.

Above right: *Misericords carved by the monks under the stalls: the man driving a tractor is by Marvin Elliot, the Loch Ness Monster by Ian Lloyd-Osborne.*

Opposite: *Exquisite stained glass windows rise above the altar.*

It might seem to be a dull existence, but there is always something that needs to be done: agricultural chores to be seen to, repairs and general upgrading, wood to be gathered and chopped. The abbey accepts commissions for stained glass and makes windows for other churches and buildings, despite the rule of silence that applies throughout the year and is lifted only at Christmas.

At the end of each day there are prayers and the monks retire at 9 p.m. They have all, for their own reasons, devoted their lives to God and renounced the temptations of the everyday world which encroaches upon them, but which they have miraculously succeeded in keeping at a distance. Many would envy them their faith, and it is hard not to admire the sentiment of their motto, which is taken from the Old Testament prophet Haggai: 'I will give peace.'

Quadripartite rib and groin vaulting in a side chapel dating from the 13th century, in which the public may join the monks in worship.

Right: *Pluscarden Abbey looking towards the old Pilgrim's North Gate situated in the medieval wall.*

James and Carolle Irvine Robertson
at Aberfeldy

18 *Perthshire heartland*

James Irvine Robertson in his library with a portrait of 'James Irvine Robertson in another life'.

Opposite: *A selection of James's hats hang on stags' antlers decorated with a tartan plaid in the hallway. On the oak chest below is a Victorian seagull in a glass dome.*

There must be something in the Scottish psyche, more than in other nationalities perhaps, which leads Scots to want to return to their roots. Great travellers and adventurers alike, Scots have always been drawn back to the lands of their ancestors, particularly when they possess a sense of history.

The picturesque market town of Aberfeldy nestles neatly into the richly wooded north Perthshire landscape which encompasses the Sma' Glen, Bonnie Prince Charlie's escape route following the Battle of Culloden in 1746, and the scenic walkway of birch trees along the Urlar Burn leading to the Falls of Moness, made famous by Robert Burns as the Birks of Aberfeldy.

It is also, in particular, intimately associated with landed and influential Highland families, such as the Menzies clan of nearby Castle Menzies, the Campbell earls of Breadalbane at Taymouth Castle, and the Atholl Stewarts. From two of the latter families, the Stewarts of Kynachan and Garth, James Irvine Robertson traces his descent. However, as is so often the case, it was to be some years before James was able to turn this to his advantage as a writer.

Born in Stirling and educated in Edinburgh, his earliest ambition was to follow in his father's footsteps and be a solicitor. Instead, he became an advertising agent in London before progressing to being a pig farmer in North Wales, then a dairy farmer in Devon. He chronicled his experiences in two hilarious books, *Any Fool Can Be a Pig Farmer* and *Any Fool Can Be a Dairy Farmer*.

Based on Exmoor, he then embarked upon a series of comic novels throughout the 1980s. In 1986, he met and married Carolle, and a few years later they moved north. James had become the custodian of a cubic metre of family papers and he realized that they were the key to a series of books, both history and fiction, which could keep him occupied for years to come.

Carolle shopping on her bicycle is a familiar sight in the village.
Above: *A hideaway at the centre of a close-knit, vibrant community.*

Opposite: *Carolle models one of her extensive collection of colourful period hats.*

While visiting Australia in her teens, Carolle had been approached by a photographer in a Sydney lift. Recognizing the potential of her dark-eyed good looks, he took some pictures, which were published in *Vogue*. She was soon in considerable demand as a high fashion model. Before meeting James, she alternated between Australia and the South of France. She finally returned to the UK and converted a barn in Sussex before settling in Dulverton on Exmoor, where she had an antique shop specializing in lace and old costume. It was there that she met James.

When they decided to seek out a suitable town or village in the Highlands, there was one simple requirement – a fresh vegetable shop a bike-ride away, for Carolle does not drive.

Aberfeldy, of course, had this to offer and so much more. Largely dependent for employment upon the surrounding farmland, the distillery that takes its name from the town, and the influx of tourists throughout the summer months, this is an active and friendly community. Carolle, with her flair for collecting and antiques, soon found herself becoming involved with charitable initiatives and thrift shops, and now notably organizes the town's annual Tradecraft Fashion Parade.

The Irvine Robertsons moved to Aberfeldy on New Year's Day 1991, coinciding more or less, as it happened, with the launch of Heartland FM, which broadcasts to Highland Perthshire from nearby Pitlochry. This was a natural outlet for James's talent, and since then he has hosted history and literature programmes as well as the weekly Roots Conversation, which explores the memories and opinions of local residents and passing celebrities. 'We flag down anyone interesting passing up or down the A9,' says James with a grin. 'Coming to Aberfeldy, the last thing I expected was to have the chance of questioning national politicians and the last thing they expect is to be gently roasted on the smallest radio station in Britain!'

In addition to this, James has found time to write local history books, the excellent *The Lady of Kynechan* (based on his ancestors during the 1745 Uprising), two anthologies for *The Field* and *Shooting Times*, and he has recently completed a biography of Major General David Stewart of Garth, a contemporary and friend of Sir Walter Scott, whose *Sketches of the Highlands*, published in 1822, underpins every subsequent book on the customs and traditions of the clans. The General is responsible for the

image of the tartan-clad Scot that has been adopted by émigrés throughout the world.

James says his next project is a novel based on the life of Isobel Mackenzie, a feisty Scottish girl who ran off with a soldier when she was 14, and before her next birthday lived consecutively with a sergeant, a captain, a colonel and an earl. She was present at the Battle of Fontenoy and, with her earl, was at Culloden. Having finally taken a husband, she made him join the Black Watch and took off with him to North America where she found herself fighting Red Indians and the French. Having given birth to 22 children, she ended her days running a pub in Tomintoul and passing travellers were still remarking on her good looks and sympathetic manner when she was in her seventies.

'That is the joy of people from this part of the world,' says James. 'There are so many extraordinary tales passed on through the generations. My forebears came from this glorious part of the Highlands – Robertsons, Irvines and Stewarts – so I'm a kind of a local, which makes it even better.'

Opposite: *Miniatures, jewelry and collectibles are displayed in a drawer hung on the wall.*

Above left: *A pageboy dumb waiter holds three of James's antiquarian books.*

Above right: *An alcove with an antique clock, collectibles and a miniature.*

Left: *An imposing oil portrait of one of Carolle's ancestors hangs in the drawing room. The chair on the right is covered in antique leopard skin.*

Top left: *Aspidistras and plants in a window.* Top right: *Carolle uses the Georgian-style doll's house as a storage cupboard.* Above: *A tea dress c. 1900 on a model beside a portrait of John Stewart of Garth, James's ancestor.*

James interviews Captain Ben Coutts, veteran 'country matters' broadcaster and author, for Radio Heartland.

Right: *An overview of the town of Aberfeldy on the River Tay looking towards Farragon on the left.*

Lord and Lady Macdonald
at Kinloch Lodge

19 *A gourmet school for the Hebrides*

Lord and Lady Macdonald at home on Skye.

Opposite: *Kinloch Lodge, which the Macdonalds run as a gourmet Highlands hotel. The statue work in the foreground to the right is by the local sculptor Lawrence Brodrick.*

The island of Skye is the second largest of the Hebrides, separated from the mainland by a narrow channel only a third of a mile wide at Kylerhea. Its extreme length is 49 miles, and its width varies between 7 and 25 miles but, because of the exceptional number of bays and inlets, no part of the island is further than 4 miles from the sea.

Skye has a land area of 643 square miles, a permanent population of approximately 7,500 and is approached by car ferry links at Glenelg/Kylerhea during the summer months, and Armadale/Mallaig throughout the year. Its accessibility was greatly enhanced in 1996 by the building of the Skye Bridge, spanning the sea between Kyleakin to Kyle of Lochalsh on the mainland.

Up until then it was always the ocean that was the high road between the land masses of the Hebrides, and throughout their history there was one clan in particular which dominated these seaways, fighting off the Viking longboats in the early part of the first millennium, policing the western seaboard as Lords of the Isles, and ultimately capitulating to the Scottish crown in the devastating battle of Bloody Bay in 1493.

For a thousand years Clan Donald has been at the heart of Scotland's Highland history, its fortunes changing in the cauldron of power. From its great ancestor Somerled in the 11th century sprang nine distinct branches. Seven survive to this day, with Godfrey Macdonald of Macdonald, 8th Lord Macdonald, recognized as High Chief and retaining his hereditary status of Ceannas nan Gaidheal, 'Headship of the Gael'.

Godfrey, a chartered accountant by training, inherited the title on the death of his father in 1970. Shortly afterwards, he and his wife Claire established Kinloch Lodge as a small country hotel while bringing up their four children, Alexandra, Isabella, Meriel and Hugo.

With ten guest bedrooms, open fires, and walls hung with ancestral portraits, their intention has always been to create a welcoming and relaxing atmosphere at the Lodge. But what has significantly helped them

to achieve this is the international recognition and the growing reputation of Claire Macdonald, an award-winning cookery writer.

As a magazine and newspaper columnist, guest speaker and demonstrator, with ten published cookery books to her credit, Claire has become a significant influence not only at Kinloch Lodge, but also on the style of many restaurants and hotels throughout Britain. At home, the emphasis is always on the freshest non-additive food from the gardens, moors and waters of Scotland, and as she became increasingly involved in food standards and presentations, it was simply a matter of time before she took her talents one step further and opened her own cookery school.

Adjacent to Kinloch Lodge, therefore, a second house called Kinloch has been purpose-built with this in mind. Kinloch – The Claire Macdonald Centre for Food and Taste, situated a 40-second walk from the Lodge, was officially opened in July 1998 with considerable support from Highlands & Island Enterprise, the government agency.

Five new bedrooms have been created, each with a spectacular view of Loch na Dal and the famous range of mountains known as the Cuillins. With a circular entrance hall, winding stone staircase, and drawing room with comfortable sofas and a 1655 refectory table, Kinloch has a specially designed kitchen, 40 x 25ft, equipped with an Aga cooker, and described by its owners as a joy to work in.

This is where Claire Macdonald provides residential cookery demonstrations throughout the year, coming up with the ideal formula for three-night residential courses which combine cookery instruction with plenty of time to relax and enjoy the break. Guests arrive the evening beforehand, in time for dinner. 'We're not sexist,' she emphasizes. 'Our courses are enjoyed as much by men as women.'

The two days that follow are broadly similar, starting off in the morning with a full demonstration, which those who know a little about what they are doing will be relieved to hear comprises not so much instruction as a series of ideas, advice on potential pitfalls, and timesaving tips which Claire has learned for herself over the years.

Kinloch Lodge sits on the shores of Loch na Dal on the eastern seaboard of Skye. The Claire Macdonald cooking school next door was officially opened in 1998.

All her demonstrations have a seasonal theme. In the autumn, for example, she might cover such topics as savoury and sweet recipes using apples, pears and nuts; game and root vegetable cooking; and preparing for Christmas.

After the cookery sessions and a late lunch, guests are encouraged to explore Skye, join an organized walk or visit Talisker, the local distillery. In the evenings, everybody gathers for pre-dinner drinks and a five-course dinner accompanied by much merriment.

Living on Skye, the 'Misty Isle', is a constant source of distraction. To the south is Armadale Castle, one-time ancestral home of the Macdonalds of Skye. Within its grounds is the Clan Donald Centre, where the full history of the clan is on display. On the same road is the Gaelic college of Sabhal Mor Ostaig. In the north-west is Dunvegan Castle, seat of Clan Macleod, who first built a defensive fort here in the 9th century. In the far north is the natural rock fortress of The Quiraing within whose recesses

Below: *The drawing room at Kinloch Lodge.*

Below right: *Claire Macdonald makes preparations for a cookery demonstration.*

A gourmet school for the Hebrides

The framed family tree shows, in part:

Somerled, Lord of the Isles = Ragnhilda daughter of Olaf the Red

Dugald · Ranald · Berthag · Angus

Donald · Ruairi

Angus Mor · Alastair Mor

Alastair Og · John Sprangach · Angus Og = Agnes O'Cahan

Amie MacRuairi = John = Margaret Stewart

Donald = Lady Margaret Leslie

Alexander

THE LINEAGE
OF THE MACDONALDS OF SLEAT

Elizabeth Seton = Daughter of Macphee = Alexander = Daughter of Gilpatrick Roy

John · Celestine of Lochalsh · Fynvola = Hugh of Sleat = Elizabeth Gunn

John · Donald Gallach = Agnes

Catherine = Donald Grumach

Margaret = Donald Gorm · John Og · Archibald the Clerk · James of the Castle

Donald Gormson = Mary

Mary = Donald Gorm Mor · Archibald, also called the Clerk

PER MARE PER TERRAS

Donald Gorm Og = Janet Mackenzie

Margaret = Sir James Mor · Donald of Castleton

Sir Donald = Margaret Douglas

Mary · Sir Donald · Sir James of Oromsay = Janet

Sir Donald · Margaret Montgomery = Sir Alexander

Sir James · Sir Alexander = Elizabeth Diana Bosville

Alexander Wentworth · Louisa Maria La Coast = Godfrey Macdonald Bosville

Alexander William Bosville · Maria Anne = Godfrey William Wentworth

Somerled · Louisa Jane Ross = Ronald Archibald

Helen Banks = Godfrey Evan Hugh

Alexander Godfrey = Anne Queenie Whitaker

Janet · Claire Catlow = Godfrey James · Archibald

Alexandra Louisa · Isabella Claire · Meriel Iona · Godfrey Evan Hugo Thomas

Above left: *A framed family tree showing the lineage of the Macdonalds of Sleat.*

Above: *Copy of a painting (the original is in the Tate Gallery) showing two of the 18th century Macdonald forebears. The boys are wearing tartan during the period after the 1745 Jacobite Uprising, when the wearing of tartan and Highland dress was banned by law.*

Overleaf: *Panoramic view of Loch na Dal.*

cattle and families were protected during the forays of Norse times, and to the south past the Storr from here is the capital of Skye, Portree, with the small islands of Raasay and Scalpay lingering to the east.

Ultimately the mythology of Skye is inextricably linked with that of Flora MacDonald from South Uist, one of the islands to the west. Kin to the then Macdonald Chief who had not supported the Jacobites, for three heady days and nights in June 1746 she helped the fugitive Prince Charles Edward Stuart to escape capture by the British troops who had decimated his army at Culloden. Their adventure is commemorated in what has become the best-known, most haunting and poignantly romantic of all Scots ballads, *The Skye Boat Song.*

The family of Macdonald has come a long way since then, and although the ancient clan lands have largely been dispersed, with clansfolk scattered globally, the enterprise of the present Chief and his talented wife has added a colourful chapter to a saga which in many ways comprises the core history of the Western Isles.

A gourmet school for the Hebrides

Sebastian and Henrietta Thewes
at Strathgarry

20 *Music in Blair Atholl*

Sebastian and Henrietta Thewes contemplate their sundial at Strathgarry.

Opposite: *Deep in the glen below Ben-y-Vrackie is the farm steading at Strathgarry which they have transformed into a mecca of music for the surrounding Perthshire communities.*

The landscape here in north Perthshire is rich and beautiful where the River Garry winds its way through Glen Garry to Tummel, below the Pass of Killiecrankie. Here, in 1689, the Jacobites won perhaps their greatest victory, but lost their commander, John Graham of Claverhouse, immortalized in song as the legendary Bonnie Dundee.

Sebastian and Henrietta Thewes moved to Strathgarry to make it their family home in 1977. But it was the acquisition ten years later of the adjacent farm steading that was to open up a whole range of possibilities for them. It was a ruin. The central part comprised a flat below a grain-store. Their original plan was to reconstruct the flat and turn the grainstore into a long, low-ceilinged room for small conferences, seminars and receptions. However, when this area was gutted and re-roofed, they were looking at a huge, beautiful, high-ceilinged room, and decided for reasons of innovation and economy to keep it like that.

It happened that the building work coincided with a visit from a good friend, Simon Wynberg, the classical guitarist. He and Sebastian, a lover of classical music, had often talked of the possibility of starting a music festival for the surrounding area with its largely rural and scattered communities; and again coincidence took a hand. That same year, Henrietta was approached for help in raising money for the Royal Marsden Hospital in London, so Simon suggested they hold a concert and dinner.

That was how it started. Simon had recently made a CD with the flautist William Bennett, known in musical circles as 'Wibb', and persuaded him to divert from New York, where he was performing, on his way to Tokyo, to play at Strathgarry on Saturday, 11 August 1990. He and Simon arrived on 9 August and began rehearsals in the house. In the meantime, invitations were sent out, and much to the Thewes' amazement and delight, it was a sell-out.

There was more good fortune to follow. Wibb, while rehearsing in the steading, had said to Sebastian, 'My boy, its just like the Wigmore Hall

Trophy heads on a wall in the bathroom which is papered in the Royal Stuart tartan.

Right: *Fishing rods and sticks in the entrance hall, and a portrait by one of the daughters of the house.*

Opposite: *The drawing room with bay window.*

when it's empty,' and asked if he might return at a later date to make a recording. Better still, he volunteered to come back and give another concert with the famous harpsichordist George Malcolm. These were the catalysts that led to the series of concerts and music festivals that were to follow.

Thus the first Music in Blair Atholl Festival was launched in 1991. As artistic director, with his contacts in the music world, Simon proved invaluable. Lavinia Gordon from nearby Lude, an accomplished musician

Left: *An eclectic collection of items, including a bass and fishing net in the entrance hall.*

Right: *Malaysia-born Bobby Chen, formerly of the Yehudi Menuhin School, who has studied with Ruth Nye at the Royal Academy of Music in London, gives a recital of piano music by J.S. Bach.*

herself, became administrator, and Colin Stephen, a friend of Paul Coletti, the viola player, who performed in the first festival and returned to Strathgarry in 1998 to get married, established them with a recording engineer.

Meanwhile, ably assisted by her sister Bumble who lives close by, Henrietta launched into a series of catering triumphs, to the extent that Derek Cooper, one of Britain's most distinguished food writers, has featured them in one of his pace-setting television documentaries. The concert hall also functions as a conference and meeting room, and for corporate entertainment, with Henrietta and Bumble providing the catering.

Another important link has been with the Surrey-based Yehudi Menuhin School – the great violinist himself became a patron of Music in Blair Atholl. Every February, students from the school come to Strathgarry

A wrought-iron gate leads into the walled garden, which was laid out early in the 19th century.
Right top: *A turret bedroom in Strathgarry House seen through the trees.* Right bottom: *A tree house built for the children.*

for their half-term holiday. As they comprise various nationalities, such as Chinese, Korean and Russian, it is not always feasible for them to go home for the holiday, and a few days spent in the countryside at Strathgarry provides a pleasant option. In the majority piano students, they hold master classes, offer tuition for local children, and give a concert at the end of the week.

Strathgarry House in its setting.

In the space of ten years, Music in Blair Atholl has been established with a considerable reputation, as well as providing a much-appreciated diversion not only for music lovers who live nearby, but for others who are prepared to drive the distance from Edinburgh, Perth, Dundee and Inverness. And it all began with the restoration of a farm steading.

The rich rolling farm-lands of Strathgarry surround this quiet glen within the Vale of Atholl.

In traditional manner, the haggis is piped into dinner for the Burns Supper. Until recently, these were all-male occasions, but women are now welcomed to speak up for themselves.

21 *A Burns Night party*

The tradition of the Burns Supper, held annually to commemorate the birth of Scotland's national bard on 25 January 1759, sprang from Lowlands Ayrshire, where he spent his childhood days. But Robert Burns's father, William Burnes, who exercised a profound influence upon his son's upbringing and education, was born in Kincardineshire, and there is much that is Highland in the ploughman poet's outlook on life. For example, his doomed relationship with Mary Cameron from Dunoon, and her early death in 1786, led to one of his most poignant works, *Highland Mary.*

Robert's humble origins, coupled with the Scottish folk tradition he helped to establish, were to raise him to icon status in his own lifetime, but even more after his early death at the age of 37. The creation of Burns societies, and the mass emigration of Scots to the New World in the centuries that followed, gave his work an international platform. Today the Burns Supper is celebrated wherever there is a gathering of Scots, or those with a love and knowledge of Scotland, throughout the world.

When Hans and Monique Baumann took up residence at Blair Mhor House in Aberdeenshire, a Burns Supper was high on their social agenda.

Traditionally, the evening starts with a piper leading guests to the dining table, whereupon he is rewarded with a dram or measure of Scotch whisky. The first course will usually consist of Cock-a-leekie soup, made from a fowl boiled with leeks, or turnips. The main course comprises haggis, neeps (mashed turnips), and tatties (mashed potatoes).

This is preceded by a formal rendition of Burns's *Address to the Haggis,* usually delivered by the host with the haggis placed in front of him on a salver. Having reached the third verse, he plunges a knife into the skin to expose its contents with the words, 'Oh, what a glorious sight, Warm-reekin, rich!'

The pudding course is variable, although Atholl Brose, a mixture of Scotch honey and oats whipped up in thick cream and a dash of Scotch,

The traditional Toast to the Haggis, 'Fair fa' your honest, sonsie face, Great Chieftain o' the puddin' race!', a high spot of every Burns Supper.

is a tradition. Wine is often served, although it is certainly the custom to provide a single malt whisky with each course, additionally or on its own.

After-dinner speeches and toasts follow, the most important being 'The Immortal Memory', where a guest will pay tribute to Robert Burns and his legacy. As the bard was known for his attraction to the ladies, this is usually followed with the 'Toast to the Lassies', then a 'Reply on behalf of the Lassies'.

The evening closes with readings from some of Burns's timeless masterpieces, such as *Tam O'Shanter* and *Holy Willy's Prayer*, and a chorus of his songs: *Ae Fond Kiss, My Love Is Like a Red Red Rose,* and the like.

Select Bibliography

HOUSES OPEN TO THE PUBLIC

Since all the homes in this book are privately owned and lived in, the authors would ask that the privacy of the individual owners is respected. However, four of the larger houses featured are open to the public on a regular basis. The details are as follows:

Inveraray Castle, Inveraray, Argyll
Open: early April to Mid-October, Monday to Thursday. Saturdays and Sundays. Open Fridays during July and August.

Ballindalloch Castle, Ballindalloch, Aberdeenshire
Open: April to September, daily

Duart Castle, Isle of Mull, Argyll
Open: May to September, daily

Torosay Castle and Gardens, Craignure, Isle of Mull, Argyll
Castle Open: April to Mid-October. Seven days.
Gardens Open: April to Mid-October. Seven days.
Winter. Open thoughout daylight hours. Seven days.

It is advisable to check opening times locally before making a visit.

Adam, Robert, and James Adam, *The Works in Architecture,* London 1975 (reprint).

Adam, William, *Vitruvius Scoticus,* Edinburgh 1980 (reprint).

Astaire Lesley, Roddy Martine and Fritz von der Schulenberg, *Living in Scotland,* London 1987.

Beard, Geoffrey, *The Work of Robert Adam,* Edinburgh 1978.

Binney, Marcus, John Harris and Emma Winnington, *Lost Houses of Scotland,* London 1980.

Cantlie, Hugh, *Ancestral Castles of Scotland,* London 1992.

Fenwick, Hubert, *Scotland's Castles,* London 1976.

Fennwick, Hubert, *Scotland's Historic Buildings,* London 1974.

Forman, Sheila, *Scotland's Country Houses and Castles,* Glasgow 1967.

Gifford, John, *The Buildings of Scotland: Highlands and Islands,* London 1992.

Irvine Robertson, James, *The First Highlander - Major General David Stewart of Garth CB, 1768-1829,* East Linton 1998.

Laing, Gerald, *Kinkell - The Reconstruction of a Scottish Castle,* Ross-shire 1984 (second edition).

Lindsay, Ian G., and Mary Cosh, *Inveraray and the Dukes of Argyll,* Edinburgh 1973.

Macaulay, James, *The Classical Country House in Scotland,* London 1987.

MacGibbon, David and Thomas Ross, *The Castellated and Domestic Architecture of Scotland,* Edinburgh 1887-92 (5 volumes).

Maclean, Charles and Christopher Simon Sykes, *Scottish Country,* London 1992.

Maclean, Fitzroy, *A Concise History of Scotland,* London 1970.

McWilliam, Colin, *The Buildings of Scotland,* London 1978.

Martine, Roddy. *Scottish Clan and Family Names - Arms, Origins & Tartans,* Edinburgh 1998 (fourth edition).

Martine, Roddy, with Patrick Douglas Hamilton, *Scotland - the Land and the Whisky,* London 1994.

Moncreiffe of that Ilk, Sir Iain Bt, *The Highland Clans,* London 1982 (fourth edition).

Montgomery-Massingberd, Hugh (ed.) *Lord of the Dance: A Moncreiffe Miscellany,* London 1986.

Montgomery-Massingberd, Hugh, with Christopher Simon Sykes, *Great Houses of Scotland,* London 1997.

Pattullo, Nan, *Castles, Houses and Gardens of Scotland,* Edinburgh 1967.

Sutherland, Douglas, *The Landowners,* London 1988 (second edition).

Sutherland, Elizabeth, *Ravens and Black Rain - The Story of Highland Second Sight,* London 1985.

Sunset over Crovie Pier,
Banffshire

Index